LEANNA   SMITH

New Mission Praise

Compiled by
Peter Horrobin and Greg Leavers

MUSIC EDITION

Marshall Pickering
An Imprint of HarperCollins*Publishers*

Marshall Pickering is an imprint of
HarperCollins*Religious*
Part of HarperCollins*Publishers*
77-85 Fulham Palace Road,
Hammersmith, London W6 8JB

First published in Great Britain
in 1996 by Marshall Pickering

1   3   5   7   9   10   8   6   4   2

A catalogue record for this book is
available from the British Library

ISBN 0 551 03013 5

Words Edition ISBN 0 551 03014 3

Music and text set by Barnes Music Engraving Ltd, East Sussex, England

Printed and bound in Great Britain by
HarperCollins*Manufacturing*, Glasgow

Preface

Mission Praise has grown in popularity because in each edition we have been able to reflect what is happening in Christian music by selecting those items which are truly 'the best of the old and the best of the new'. Over the past few years there has been a wealth of new music available and selecting those items which are more than ephemeral has been a fascinating task.

Music is such an integral part of worship that we must always be open to allow our horizons to be stretched by trying music that has blessed others - even if it does not come from our own favourite tradition! We pray that the selection of more contemporary Christian music will encourage you to try new material if you are not already familiar with it.

Conversely, we are also delighted to include some much older items which have either gained in popularity in recent years, or which had to be omitted, for reasons of space, from earlier editions.

It is our prayer that this new volume will be both an encouragement and an inspiration to all who enjoy using **Mission Praise** in their services of praise and worship.

Peter Horrobin and Greg Leavers

1

All I once held dear
(Knowing You)

Words and music: Graham Kendrick

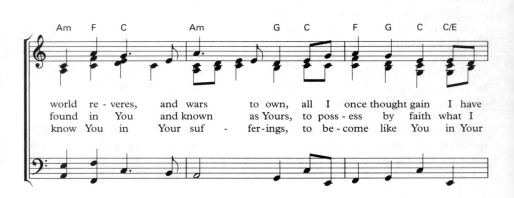

1 All I once held dear, built my life up-on, all this
(2) heart's de-sire is to know You___ more, to be
(3) know the power of Your ri-sen___ life, and to

world re-veres, and wars to own, all I once thought gain I have
found in You and known as Yours, to poss-ess by faith what I
know You in Your suf-fer-ings, to be-come like You in Your

coun-ted_ loss; spent and worth-less now, com-pared to this:
could not earn, all-sur-pass-ing gift of right-eous-ness. *Know-ing*
death, my Lord, so with You to live and ne-ver die.

You, Je-sus, know-ing You, there is no great - er

thing. You're my all, You're the best, You're my

joy, my right-eous-ness, and I love You, Lord. 2 Now my
3 Oh, to

love You, Lord, love You, Lord.

2

All-consuming, all-embracing

Words and music: Chris Bowater

All-con-sum-ing, ___ all-em-brac-ing, fer-vent God of love, en-thral me. All-con-sum-ing, ___ all-em-brac-ing, fer-vent God_ of love, en-thral me, 'til all that I am and I de-

- sire   is   whol - ly,   on - ly____ owned,   con-

- trolled   by   You.

All-consuming, all-embracing,
fervent God of love, enthral me.
All-consuming, all-embracing,
fervent God of love, enthral me,
'til all that I am and I desire
is wholly, only owned, controlled by You.

3

All that I am
(I offer my life)

Words and music: Claire Cloninger
and Don Moen

1 All that I am,___ all that I have,___
2 Things in the past,___ things yet un - seen,___

I lay them down be-fore You,___ O Lord; all my re - grets,
wish-es and dreams that are yet___ to come true; all of my hopes,

all my ac - claim, the joy and the pain, I'm mak - ing them Yours.
all of my plans, my heart and my hands are lift - ed to You.

Lord, I of - fer my life___ to You, ev - ery-thing I've

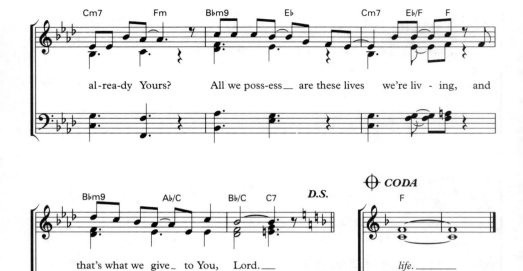

al-rea-dy Yours? All we poss-ess__ are these lives we're liv - ing, and

that's what we give_ to You, Lord.__

CODA

life._____

1 All that I am, all that I have,
   I lay them down before You, O Lord;
   all my regrets, all my acclaim,
   the joy and the pain,
   I'm making them Yours.
        Lord, I offer my life to You,
        everything I've been through—
        use it for Your glory.
        Lord, I offer my days to You,
        lifting my praise to You
        as a pleasing sacrifice:
        Lord, I offer You my life.

2 Things in the past, things yet unseen,
   wishes and dreams that are yet to come true;
   all of my hopes, all of my plans,
   my heart and my hands
   are lifted to You.
        Lord, I offer my life to You . . .

   What can we give that You have not given,
   and what do we have that is not already Yours?
   All we possess are these lives we're living,
   and that's what we give to You, Lord.
        Lord, I offer my life to You . . .

4

And He shall reign

Words and music: Graham Kendrick

reign   for   ev - er,   and

Fine

we   shall   reign   with   Him. _____

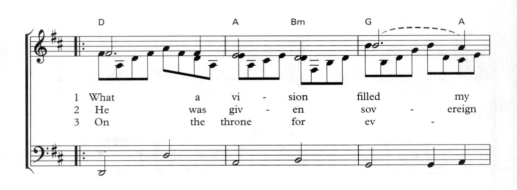

1   What   a   vi - sion   filled   my
2   He   was   giv - en   sov - ereign
3   On   the   throne   for   ev -

eyes –   one___   like   a   son   of
power,   glo - ry   and   au - tho - ri -
- er,   see   the   Lamb   who   once   was

5
As water to the thirsty

OASIS   76 76 66 446

Words: Timothy Dudley-Smith
Music: T Brian Coleman
arranged Roger Mayor

1 As wa - ter to the thir - sty, as beau - ty to the eyes,
as strength that fol - lows weak - ness, as

2 Like calm in place of clam - our, like peace that fol - lows pain,
like meet - ing af - ter part - ing, like

3 As sleep that fol - lows fe - ver, as gold in - stead of grey,
as free - dom af - ter bond - age, as

6　　Awake, my soul, and with the sun

Morning Hymn　LM

Words: Thomas Ken (1637–1711)
Music: F H Barthelemon (1741–1808)

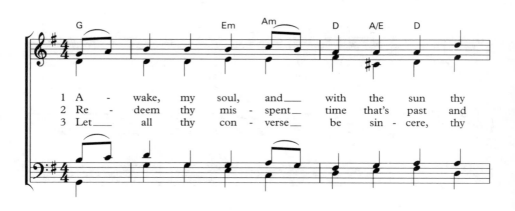

1 A - wake, my soul, and__ with the sun thy
2 Re - deem thy mis - spent__ time that's past and
3 Let__ all thy con - verse__ be sin - cere, thy

dai - ly stage of__ du - ty run; shake off dull_ sloth, and__
live this day__ as__ if thy last; im - prove thy__ ta - lent
con-science as__ the__ noon-day clear; think how all - see - ing__

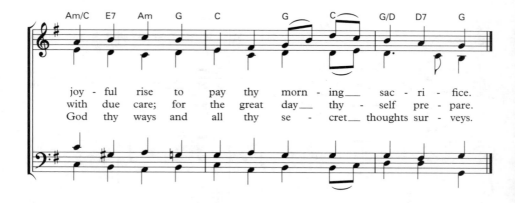

joy - ful rise to pay thy morn - ing__ sac - ri - fice.
with due care; for the great day__ thy - self pre - pare.
God thy ways and all thy se - cret__ thoughts sur - veys.

PART I

1 Awake, my soul, and with the sun
thy daily stage of duty run;
shake off dull sloth, and joyful rise
to pay thy morning sacrifice.

2 Redeem thy mis-spent time that's past
and live this day as if thy last;
improve thy talent with due care;
for the great day thyself prepare.

3 Let all thy converse be sincere,
thy conscience as the noon-day clear;
think how all-seeing God thy ways
and all thy secret thoughts surveys.

4 Wake, and lift up thyself, my heart,
and with the angels bear thy part,
who all night long unwearied sing
high praise to the eternal King.

PART II

5 Glory to thee, who safe hast kept
and hast refreshed me whilst I slept;
grant, Lord, when I from death shall wake,
I may of endless light partake.

6 Lord, I my vows to thee renew;
disperse my sins as morning dew;
guard my first springs of thought and will,
and with Thyself my spirit fill.

7 Direct, control, suggest, this day,
all I design or do or say;
that all my powers, with all their might,
in Thy sole glory may unite.

DOXOLOGY
(may be sung after either part)

Praise God, from whom all blessings flow,
praise Him, all creatures here below,
praise Him above, angelic host,
praise Father, Son and Holy Ghost.

7 At the foot of the cross

Words and music: Derek Bond

free;_____ and I will give my life___ to You,___ dear Lord, and

praise Your maj - es - ty,_____ and praise Your maj - es -

- ty,_____ and praise Your maj - es - ty._____

At the foot of the cross—
I can hardly take it in
that the King of all creation
was dying for my sin.
Oh, the pain and agony
and the thorns that pierced Your head,
and the hardness of my sinful heart
that left You there for dead!

And oh, what mercy I have found
at the cross of Calvary!
I will never know Your loneliness,
all on account of me.
And I will bow my knee before Your throne,
for Your love has set me free;
and I will give my life to You, dear Lord,
and praise Your majesty,
and praise Your majesty,
and praise Your majesty.

8

Beauty for brokenness
(God of the poor)

Words and music: Graham Kendrick

Thoughtfully ♩ = 120

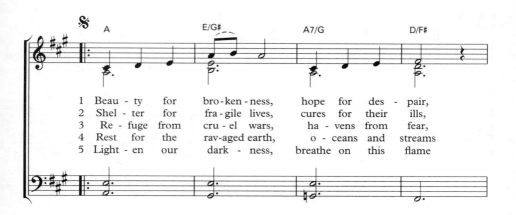

1 Beau - ty for bro - ken - ness, hope for des - pair,
2 Shel - ter for fra - gile lives, cures for their ills,
3 Re - fuge from cru - el wars, ha - vens from fear,
4 Rest for the rav-aged earth, o - ceans and streams
5 Light - en our dark - ness, breathe on this flame

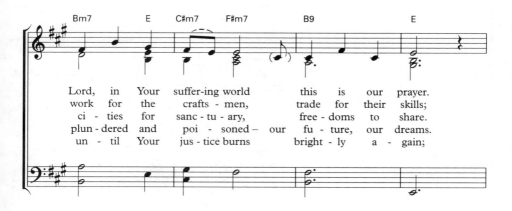

Lord, in Your suffer-ing world this is our prayer.
work for the crafts - men, trade for their skills;
ci - ties for sanc - tu - ary, free - doms to share.
plun - dered and poi - soned — our fu - ture, our dreams.
un - til Your jus - tice burns bright - ly a - gain;

9 Behold the Lord

From Revelation 4
Words and music: Noel Richards
and Gerald Coates

With strength

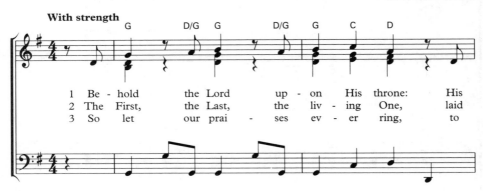

1 Be - hold the Lord up - on His throne: His
2 The First, the Last, the liv - ing One, laid
3 So let our prai - ses ev - er ring, to

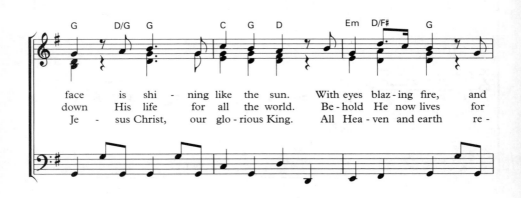

face is shi - ning like the sun. With eyes blaz - ing fire, and
down His life for all the world. Be - hold He now lives for
Je - sus Christ, our glo - rious King. All Hea - ven and earth re -

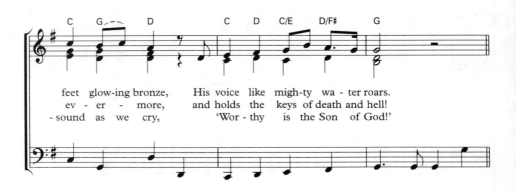

feet glow-ing bronze, His voice like migh-ty wa - ter roars.
ev - er - more, and holds the keys of death and hell!
- sound as we cry, 'Wor - thy is the Son of God!'

Ho - ly, ho - ly, Lord God al - migh-ty:
Ho - ly, ho - ly, Lord God al - migh-ty:
Ho - ly, ho - ly, Lord God al - migh-ty:

ho - ly, ho - ly! We stand in awe of You.
ho - ly, ho - ly! We bow be - fore Your throne.
ho - ly, ho - ly! We fall down at Your feet.

1 Behold the Lord upon His throne:
His face is shining like the sun.
With eyes blazing fire,
and feet glowing bronze,
His voice like mighty water roars.
    Holy, holy, Lord God almighty:
    holy, holy! We stand in awe of You.

2 The First, the Last, the living One,
laid down His life for all the world.
Behold He now lives for evermore,
and holds the keys of death and hell!
    Holy, holy, Lord God almighty:
    holy, holy! We bow before Your throne.

3 So let our praises ever ring,
to Jesus Christ, our glorious King.
All Heaven and earth resound as we cry,
'Worthy is the Son of God!'
    Holy, holy, Lord God almighty:
    holy, holy! We fall down at Your feet.

10 Blessèd be the name of the Lord

From Psalm 18
Words and music: Danny Daniels
and Kevin Prosch

He   is our rock,   for He   is our
u - ni - verse____   is in   the hands

rock,_____ He is the Lord.   For
_____ of the Lord.___   The

He   is our rock,   for He   is our
u - ni - verse____   is in   the hands

rock,_____ He is the Lord.
_____ of the Lord.___

11 Blessèd be the name of the Lord

From Proverbs 18
Words and music: Clinton Utterbach
Music arranged Christopher Norton

12

By Your side

Words and music: Noel and Tricia Richards

13

Called to a battle
(Thunder in the skies)

Words and music: Noel and Tricia Richards
arranged I Hannah

14

Christ is risen

Words and music: Chris Rolinson

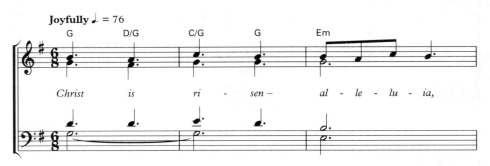

Christ is ri - sen – al - le - lu - ia,

al - le - lu - ia! Christ is ri - sen –

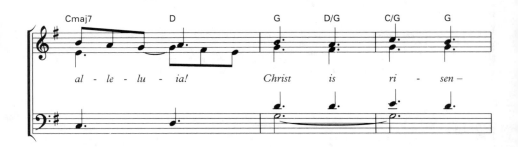

ri - sen in - deed, al - le - lu - ia!

Fine

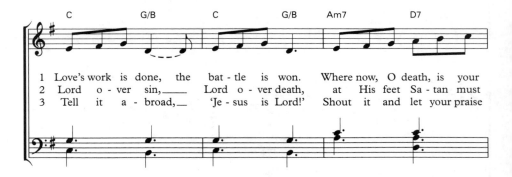

1 Love's work is done, the bat - tle is won. Where now, O death, is your
2 Lord o - ver sin,___ Lord o - ver death, at His feet Sa - tan must
3 Tell it a - broad,___ 'Je - sus is Lord!' Shout it and let your praise

sting?   He rose a - gain   to   rule and to reign,
fall!   Ev - ery knee bow!   All will con - fess
ring!   Glad - ly we raise   our songs of praise –

D.C. al Fine

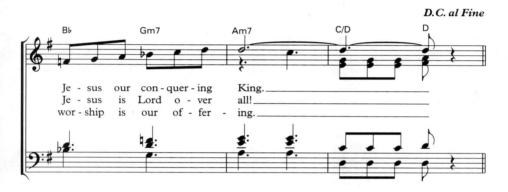

Je - sus our con - quer - ing   King.
Je - sus is Lord o - ver   all!
wor - ship is our of - fer - ing.

Christ is risen–
alleluia, alleluia!
Christ is risen–
risen indeed, alleluia!

1 Love's work is done,
 the battle is won.
 Where now, O death, is your sting?
 He rose again
 to rule and to reign,
 Jesus our conquering King.
  Christ is risen . . .

2 Lord over sin,
 Lord over death,
 at His feet Satan must fall!
 Every knee bow!
 All will confess
 Jesus is Lord over all!
  Christ is risen . . .

3 Tell it abroad,
 'Jesus is Lord!'
 Shout it and let your praise ring!
 Gladly we raise
 our songs of praise–
 worship is our offering.
  Christ is risen . . .

15   Christom is the One who calls

LOVE UNKNOWN   66 66 44 44

Words: Timothy Dudley-Smith
Music: John Ireland (1879–1962)
arranged Christopher Norton

1 Christ is the One who calls, the One who loved and
2 Christ is the One who seeks, to whom our souls are
3 Christ is the One who died, for - sak - en and be-

came, to whom by right it falls to bear the high - est
known. The word of love He speaks can wake a heart of
-trayed; who, mocked and cru - ci - fied, the price of par - don

An SATB arrangement for this tune will be found at *Combined Mission Praise* 478.

name: and still to - day_____ our hearts are
stone; for at that sound_____ the blind can
paid. Our dy - ing Lord,_____ what grief and

stirred to hear His word and walk His way.
see, the slave is free, the lost are found.
loss, what bit - ter cross our souls re - stored!

4 Christ is the One who rose
  in glory from the grave,
  to share His life with those
  whom once He died to save.
    He drew death's sting
    and broke its chains,
    who lives and reigns
    our risen King.

5 Christ is the One who sends,
  His story to declare;
  who calls His servants friends
  and gives them news to share.
    His truth proclaim
    in all the earth,
    His matchless worth
    and saving name.

16 · City of God, how broad and far

RICHMOND   CM

Words: Samuel Johnson (1822–82)
Music: adapted from Thomas Haweis (1734–1820)
by Samuel Webbe the Younger (1770–1843)
arranged Christopher Norton

Smoothly ♩ = 104

1 Ci-ty of God, how broad_ and far out-
2 One ho-ly Church, one ar - my strong, one
3 How pure-ly hath thy speech come down from

- spread thy walls_ sub - lime! The true_____ thy
stead - fast, high_ in - tent; one work - ing
man's_ pri - me - val youth! How grand - ly

An SATB arrangement for this tune will be found at *Combined Mission Praise* 146(ii).

Music arrangement: © 1993 HarperCollins*Religious* / CopyCare Ltd,
PO Box 77, Hailsham BN27 3EF, UK. Used by permission.

char - tered free - men are of ev - ery
band,___ one har - vest - song, one King___ om -
hath___ thine em - pire grown of free - dom,

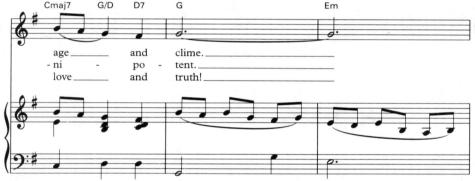

age___ and clime.___
- ni - po - tent.___
love___ and truth!___

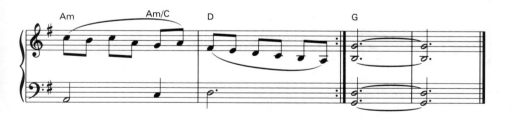

4 How gleam thy watch-fires through the night
with never-fainting ray!
How rise thy towers, serene and bright,
to meet the dawning day!

5 In vain the surge's angry shock,
in vain the drifting sands:
unharmed upon the eternal Rock
the eternal city stands.

17

Closer to You

Words and music: Trish Morgan

Clo-ser to You, Lord, and clo-ser still, 'til I am whol-ly in Your will, Clo-ser to hear Your beat-ing heart, and un-der-stand what You im-part. O Breath of life,

18 Come, let us worship Jesus
(King of the nations)

Words and music: Graham Kendrick

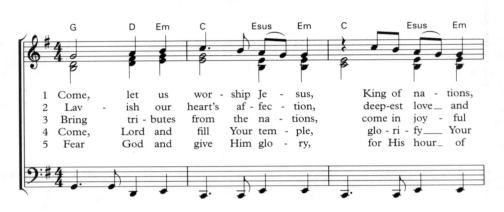

1 Come, let us wor - ship Je - sus, King of na - tions,
2 Lav - ish our heart's af - fec - tion, deep-est love and
3 Bring tri - butes from the na - tions, come in joy - ful
4 Come, Lord and fill Your tem - ple, glo - ri - fy Your
5 Fear God and give Him glo - ry, for His hour of

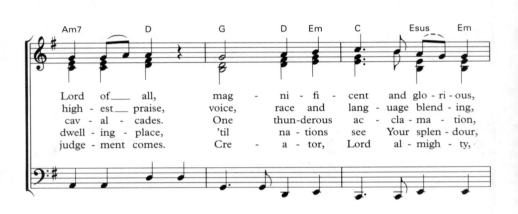

Lord of all, mag - ni - fi - cent and glo - ri - ous,
high - est praise, voice, race and lang - uage blend - ing,
cav - al - cades. One thun-derous ac - cla - ma - tion,
dwell - ing - place, 'til na - tions see Your splen - dour,
judge - ment comes. Cre - a - tor, Lord al - migh - ty,

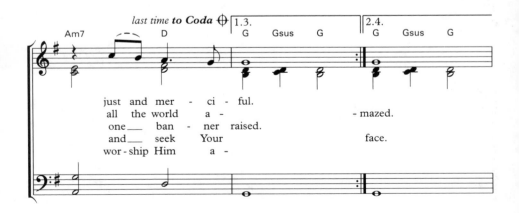

last time **to Coda**

1.3.   2.4.

just and mer - ci - ful.
all the world a - - mazed.
one ban - ner raised.
and seek Your face.
wor - ship Him a -

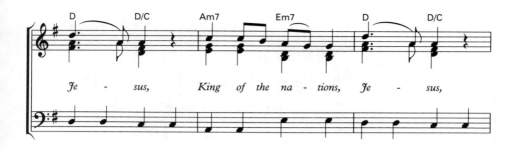

Jesus, King of the nations, Jesus,

Lord of____ all. Jesus,

King of the na - tions, Lord of_____ all!

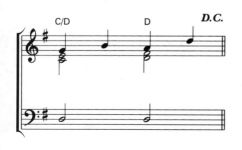

D.C.

⊕ *CODA*

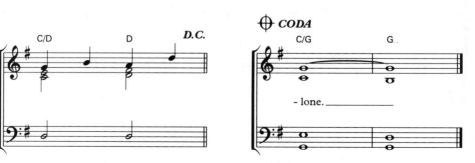

- lone._____

19 Confidence, we have confidence

Words and music: Chris Bowater

Gently, building in strength

Con - fi - dence, we have con - fi - dence

to come,_ to ask____ for

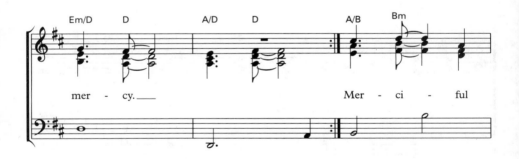

mer - cy.____ Mer - ci - ful

God, we cry, 'Don't pass us by.'___

Mer - ci - ful God, we pray, 'Don't turn a - way';

— in Your love___ re - mem - ber mer-

- cy, in Your love___ re - mem-

- ber mer - cy. ___

20 Come, Holy Spirit

Words and music: John L Bell

From the *Come All You People* collection (Wild Goose Publications, 1995)

Words and music: © 1992, 1995 WGRG Iona Community,
Pearce Institute, 840 Govan Road, Glasgow G51 3UU, Scotland, UK.

Consider how He loves you
(Sweet perfume)

Words and music: John Wimber

1 Con - si - der how＿＿＿ He loves＿ you, His arms of love＿ en - fold you like a sweet, sweet＿＿＿ per - fume.＿＿＿ He

22 Depth of mercy

WORCESTER 77 777

Words: Charles Wesley (1707–88)
Music: Richard Rance

1 Depth of mer - cy! Can there be mer - cy still re-served for me? Can my God His wrath for - bear, me, the chief of sin - ners spare, me, the chief of
2 I have long with - stood His grace, long pro - voked Him to His face, would not heark - en to His calls, grieved Him by a thou - sand falls, grieved Him by a
3 Whence to me this waste of love? Ask my ad - vo - cate a - bove; see the cause in Je - sus' face, now be - fore the throne of grace, now be - fore the
4 There for me the Sav - iour stands, shows His wounds and spreads His hands. God is love, I know, I feel, Je - sus lives and loves me still, Je - sus lives and

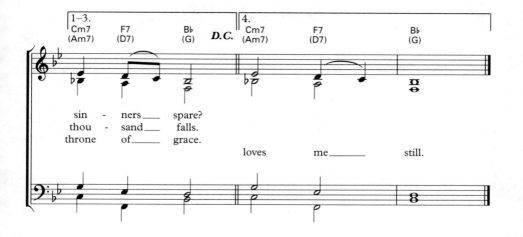

1–3.				4.		
Cm7	F7	B♭	**D.C.**	Cm7	F7	B♭
(Am7)	(D7)	(G)		(Am7)	(D7)	(G)

sin - ners___ spare?
thou - sand___ falls.
throne of___ grace.

loves   me___   still.

1 Depth of mercy! Can there be
mercy still reserved for me?
Can my God His wrath forbear,
me, the chief of sinners spare,
me, the chief of sinners spare?

2 I have long withstood His grace,
long provoked Him to His face,
would not hearken to His calls,
grieved Him by a thousand falls,
grieved Him by a thousand falls.

3 Whence to me this waste of love?
Ask my advocate above;
see the cause in Jesus' face,
now before the throne of grace,
now before the throne of grace.

4 There for me the Saviour stands,
shows His wounds and spreads His hands.
God is love, I know, I feel,
Jesus lives and loves me still,
Jesus lives and loves me still.

23 Down the mountain
(The river is here)

Words and music: Andy Park

1 Down the_ moun-tain the ri - ver_ flows, and it
2 The ri-ver of__ God is teem-ing with life, _
3 Up to the_ moun-tain we love to_ go, _

brings re - fresh-ing wher-ev-er it goes. Through the_ val - leys and
and all_ who touch it can be re - vived, and those who lin - ger on
to find the_ pres-ence of__ the Lord. A - long the_ banks of the

24

Eternal God

CHARTERHOUSE 11 10 11 10

Words: Alan Gaunt
Music: David Evans (1874–1948)

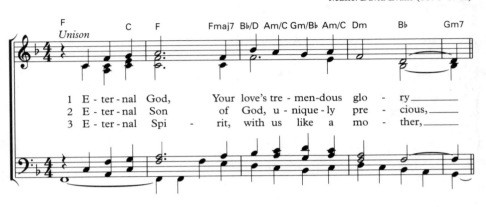

1 E-ter-nal God, Your love's tre-men-dous glo - ry_____
2 E-ter-nal Son of God, u-nique-ly pre - cious,_____
3 E-ter-nal Spi - rit, with us like a mo - ther,_____

cas-cades through life in o - ver - flow - ing grace,_____
in You, des - ert - ed, scorned and cru - ci - fied,_____
em-brac - ing us in love se - rene and pure:

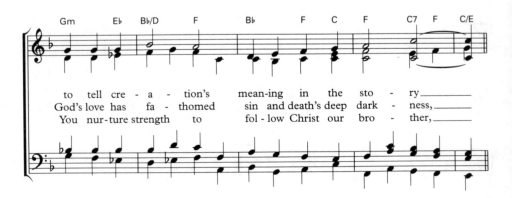

to tell cre - a - tion's mean-ing in the sto - ry_____
God's love has fa - thomed sin and death's deep dark - ness,_____
You nur-ture strength to fol - low Christ our bro - ther,_____

From the *Revised Church Hymnary*, 1927

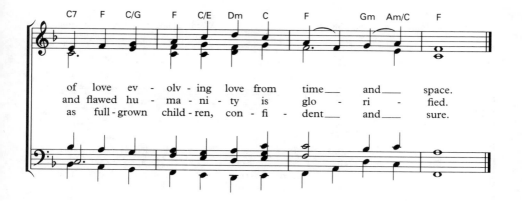

of love ev - olv - ing love from time___ and___ space.
and flawed hu - ma - ni - ty is glo - ri - fied.
as full - grown child - ren, con - fi - dent___ and___ sure.

1 Eternal God, Your love's tremendous glory
   cascades through life in overflowing grace,
   to tell creation's meaning in the story
   of love evolving love from time and space.

2 Eternal Son of God, uniquely precious,
   in You, deserted, scorned and crucified,
   God's love has fathomed sin and death's deep darkness,
   and flawed humanity is glorified.

3 Eternal Spirit, with us like a mother,
   embracing us in love serene and pure:
   You nurture strength to follow Christ our brother,
   as full-grown children, confident and sure.

4 Love's trinity, self-perfect, self-sustaining;
   love which commands, enables and obeys:
   You give Yourself, in boundless joy, creating
   one vast increasing harmony of praise.

5 We ask You now, complete Your image in us;
   this love of Yours, our source and guide and goal.
   May love in us, seek love and serve love's purpose,
   till we ascend with Christ and find love whole.

25   Fairest Lord Jesus

SCHÖNSTER HERR JESU   568 558

Words: Lilian Stevenson (1870–1960), altd
Music: Silesian folk song
arranged David Peacock

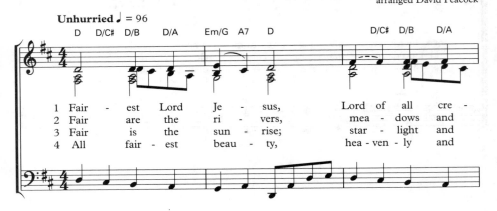

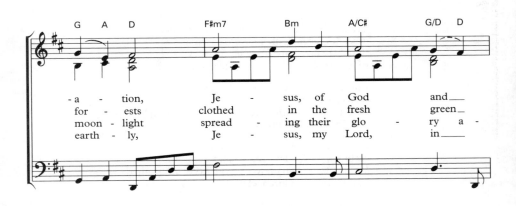

1 Fair - est Lord Je - sus, Lord of all cre -
2 Fair are the ri - vers, mea - dows and
3 Fair is the sun - rise; star - light and
4 All fair - est beau - ty, hea - ven - ly and

- a - tion, Je - sus, of God and___
for - ests clothed in the fresh green_
moon - light spread - ing their glo - ry a -
earth - ly, Je - sus, my Lord, in___

man the Son; You will I
robes of spring; Je - sus is
- cross the sky; Je - sus shines
You I see; none can be

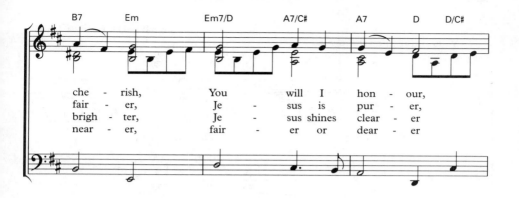

che - rish,   You   will I hon - our,
fair - er,   Je - sus is pur - er,
brigh - ter,   Je - sus shines clear - er
near - er,   fair - er or dear - er

You   are   my   soul's   de - light   and
He   makes   the   sad - dest heart   to
than   all   the   heaven - ly host   on
than   You,   my   Sav - iour, are   to

crown._____
sing._____
high._____

me.

26

Faithful God

Words and music: Chris Bowater

Faith - ful God, _____ faith - ful God, _____ all - suf - fi - cient One, I wor - ship You. _____ Sha - lom my peace, _____ my strong De - liv - er - er, I lift You up, faith - ful God. _____

Faithful One

Words and music: Brian Doerksen

Faith - ful One, so un- chang - ing;____ age - less One, You're my rock____ of____ peace. Lord of

28 Father of creation
(Let Your glory fall)

Words and music: David Ruis

1 Fa - ther___ of cre - a - tion,
2 Rul - er___ of the na - tions,

un - fold Your sov - ereign plan.___
the world has yet___ to see___

Raise up a cho - sen ge-ne-ra - tion___
the full re-lease of Your pro - mise –

29 Father of heaven, whose love profound

RIVAULX LM

Words: E Cooper (1770–1833)
Music: J B Dykes (1823–76)

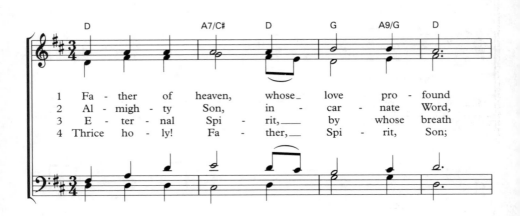

1 Fa - ther of heaven, whose_ love pro - found
2 Al - migh - ty Son, in - car - nate Word,
3 E - ter - nal Spi - rit,___ by whose breath
4 Thrice ho - ly! Fa - ther,___ Spi - rit, Son;

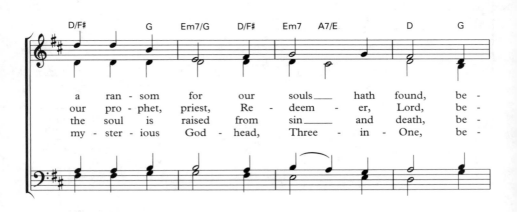

a ran - som for our souls___ hath found, be -
our pro - phet, priest, Re - deem - er, Lord, be -
the soul is raised from sin___ and death, be -
my - ster - ious God - head, Three - in - One, be -

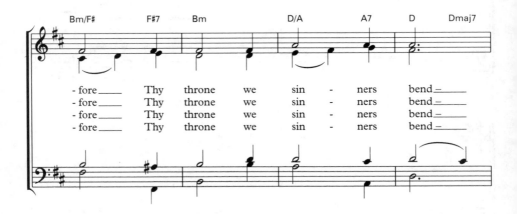

- fore___ Thy throne we sin - ners bend_
- fore___ Thy throne we sin - ners bend_
- fore___ Thy throne we sin - ners bend_
- fore___ Thy throne we sin - ners bend_

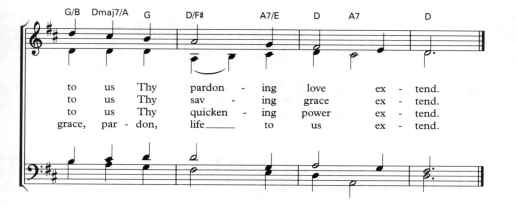

to	us	Thy	pardon - ing	love	ex -	tend.
to	us	Thy	sav - ing	grace	ex -	tend.
to	us	Thy	quicken - ing	power	ex -	tend.
grace,	par - don,		life___ to	us	ex -	tend.

1 Father of heaven, whose love profound
   a ransom for our souls hath found,
   before Thy throne we sinners bend–
   to us Thy pardoning love extend.

2 Almighty Son, incarnate Word,
   our prophet, priest, Redeemer, Lord,
   before Thy throne we sinners bend–
   to us Thy saving grace extend.

3 Eternal Spirit, by whose breath
   the soul is raised from sin and death,
   before Thy throne we sinners bend–
   to us Thy quickening power extend.

4 Thrice holy! Father, Spirit, Son;
   mysterious Godhead, Three-in-One,
   before Thy throne we sinners bend–
   grace, pardon, life to us extend.

30

Filled with compassion

Words and music: Noel and Tricia Richards

1 Filled with com-pas-sion for all cre-a-tion,
Je-sus came in-to a world that was lost.
There was but one way that He could save us,
on-ly through suf-fer-ing death on a cross.

2 Great is Your pas-sion for all the peo-ple
liv-ing and dy-ing with-out know-ing You.
Hav-ing no sav-iour, they're lost for ev-er
if we don't speak out and lead them to You.

3 From ev-ery na-tion we shall be ga-thered,
mil-lions re-deemed shall be Je-sus' re-ward.
Then He will turn and say to His Fa-ther:
'Tru-ly my suf-fer-ing was worth it all!'

31 For the joys and for the sorrows

Words and music: Graham Kendrick

1 For the joys_ and for_ the sor-rows, the best and worst of times,
2 For the tears that flow_ in se-cret, in the bro-ken times,
3 For the weak-ness of_ my bo-dy, the bur-dens of_ each day,_

for this mo-ment, for_ to-mor-row, for
for the mo-ments of_ e-la-tion,
for the nights of doubt_ and wor-ry, when

all that lies_ be-hind;_
or the trou-bled mind;_ for
sleep has fled_ a-way;_

fears that crowd a-round
all the dis-ap-point-
need-ing re-as-sur-

_ me, for the fail-ure of_ my plans,_
-ments, or the sting of old_ re-grets,_
-ance, and the will to start_ a-gain,_

for the
a

dreams of all__ I hope__ to be,__ the truth of what I am:
all my prayers and long - ings_____ that seem un - ans - wered yet:_
steel - y - eyed_ en - dur - ance,_____ the strength to fight and win:

For_ this I have Je - sus, for__

this I have Je - sus, for__ this I have Je - sus,

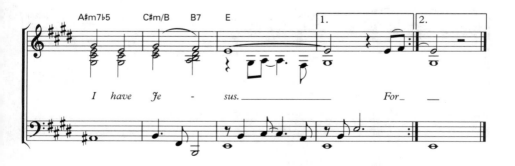

I have Je - sus. _____ For_ __

32 God has chosen me

From Luke 4
Words and music: Bernadette Farrell

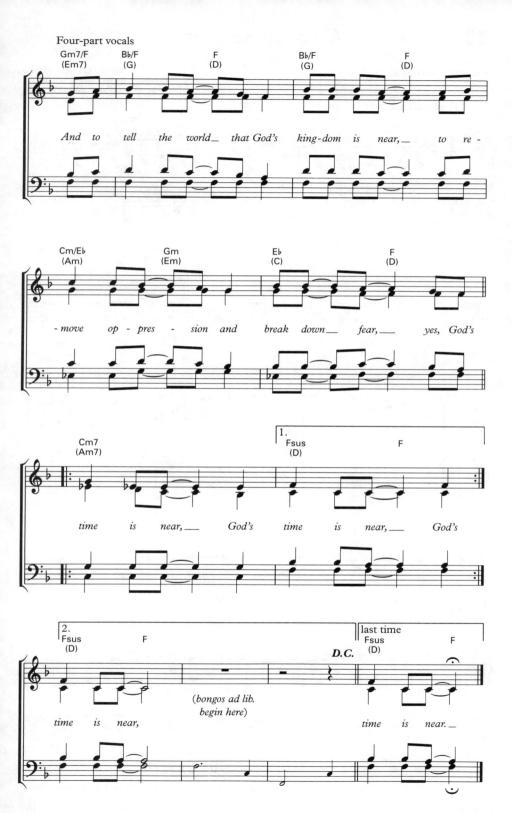

33

God has spoken

EBENEZER   87 87 D

Words: George Briggs
Music: Thomas J Williams (1869–1944)
arranged Christopher Norton

Rock ballad ♩ = 88

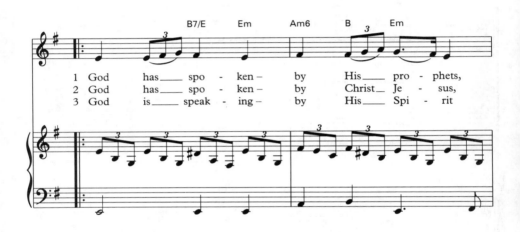

1 God has spo - ken - by His pro - phets,
2 God has spo - ken - by Christ Je - sus,
3 God is speak - ing - by His Spi - rit

spo - ken His un - chang - ing word;
Christ, the ev - er - last - ing Son;
speak - ing to our hearts a - gain;

An SATB arrangement for this tune will be found at *Combined Mission Praise* 522.

Music: © D Evans

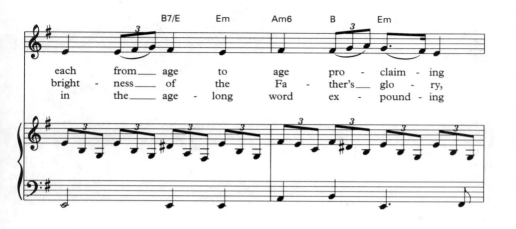

each   from___ age   to   age   pro - claim - ing

bright - ness___ of   the   Fa - ther's___ glo - ry,

in   the___ age - long   word   ex - pound - ing

God   the___ One,___ the   right - eous   Lord;

with   the___ Fa - ther   ev - er   one:

God's   own___ mes - sage,   now___ as   then.

in   the ___ world's   des - pair   and___ tur - moil

spo - ken___ by   the   Word   in - car - nate,

Through   the___ rise   and   fall   of___ na - tions

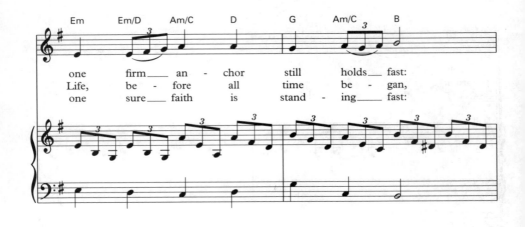

one   firm____ an - chor   still   holds____ fast:
Life,   be - fore   all   time   be - gan,
one   sure____ faith   is   stand - ing____ fast:

God   is____ King,   His   throne   e - ter - nal,
Light   of____ light   to   earth   de - scend - ing,
God   a - bides,   His   word   un - chang - ing,

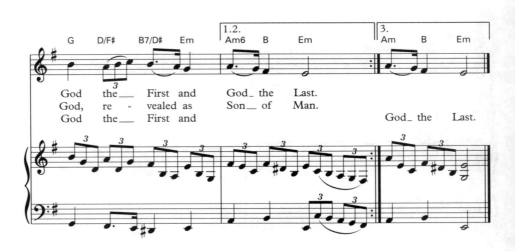

God   the____ First and   God__ the   Last.
God,   re - vealed as   Son__ of   Man.
God   the____ First and   God__ the   Last.

34 God in His love for us

STEWARDSHIP   11 10 11 10 Dactylic

Words: Fred Pratt Green
Music: Valerie Ruddle

1 God in His love for us lent us this pla - net, gave it a
2 Thanks be to God for its boun - ty and beau - ty, life that sus -
3 Long have our hu - man wars ru - ined its har - vest; long has earth
4 Earth is the Lord's: it is ours to en - joy it, ours, as His

pur - pose in time and in space: small as__ a spark from the
- tains us in bo - dy and mind: plen - ty__ for all, if we
bowed to the ter - ror of force; long have_ we wa - sted what
ste - wards, to farm and de - fend. From its__ pol - lu - tion, mis -

fire of cre - a - tion,_ cra - dle of life and the home of our race.
learn how to share it,__ rich - es un - dreamed - of to fa - thom and find.
oth - ers have need of,__ poi - soned the foun - tain of life at its source.
- use and de - struc - tion,_ good Lord de - liv - er us, world with - out end!

35 God of grace

Words and music: Chris Bowater

With feeling

1 God of grace, I turn my face to You— I can-not
2 Stri-vings and— all an-guished dreams in rags lie at my

hide; my na-ked-ness, my shame, my guilt, are
feet, and on-ly grace pro-vides the way— for

all be-fore— Your eyes.
me to stand com- -plete. And Your

grace clothes me in right - eous-

-ness, and Your mer - cy co-vers me in

love; Your life a - dorns

and beau - ti - fies I

stand com-plete in You.

36   Great is God

From Ephesians 2:4–5
Words and music: Stuart Haynes
arranged Julian A Perkins

Great is God whose mer-cy has found us, cast a - way the chains that have bound us. We can go forth in li - ber - ty, prai-sing the name of the Lord! We are free, let

hea - ven de - clare it, lift your voice, let all peo - ple share it!

We are _____ no more in sla - ve - ry ___ sing with your heart a - flame,

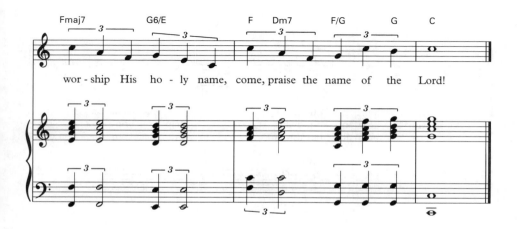

wor - ship His ho - ly name, come, praise the name of the Lord!

37

Great is the darkness
(Come, Lord Jesus)

Words and music: Gerald Coates
and Noel Richards

Growing in strength

1 Great is___ the dark-ness that co-vers the earth, op-pres-sion, in-jus-tice and
2 May now Your Church rise with po-wer and love, this glo-ri-ous gos-pel pro-
3 Great ce-le-bra-tions on that fi-nal day, when out of the hea-vens You

pain.
-claim.
come.

Na-tions are slip-ping in hope-less des-pair, though
In ev-ery na-tion sal-va-tion will come to
Dark-ness will va-nish, all sor-row will end, and

ma-ny___ have come in___ Your name,   watch-ing___ while sa-ni-ty
those who be-lieve in___ Your name.   Help us___ bring light to___ the
ru-lers will bow at___ Your throne.   Our great com-mis-sion com-

dies,   touched by_ the mad - ness and lies._____
world,   that we_ might speed Your re - turn._____
- plete,   then face to face we_ shall meet._____

Come, Lord Je - sus, come, Lord Je - sus, pour out_ Your Spi - rit, we

pray.   Come, Lord Je - sus, come, Lord Je - sus,

pour out_ Your Spi - rit on us to - day.   -day.

38

God is great

Words and music: Graham Kendrick
and Steve Thompson

God is__ great, a - maz-ing! Come, let His prai - ses ring.

God is__ great, a - stound-ing! The whole cre - a - tion

pa - lace of stars, and rides on the wings of the wind.
great and the small, He wat-ches and cares for them all.
- rag-eous, a - blaze in col-our-ful pag-eants of praise.
day fol-lows night, yet He knows ev - ery beat of my heart.
- gain and a - gain as they soar in the arch of the heavens.

✠ CODA

D.S.

sings.

God is great, amazing!
Come, let His praises ring.
God is great, astounding!
The whole creation sings.

1 His clothing is splendour and majesty bright,
   for He wraps Himself in a garment of light.
   He spreads out the heavens– His palace of stars,
   and rides on the wings of the wind.
       God is great . . .

2 What marvellous wisdom the Maker displays,
   the sea vast and spacious, the dolphins and whales,
   the earth full of creatures, the great and the small,
   He watches and cares for them all.
       God is great . . .

3 The rain forest canopies darken the skies,
   cathedrals of mist that resound with the choirs
   of creatures discordant, outrageous, ablaze
   in colourful pageants of praise.
       God is great . . .

4 Above His creation the Father presides:
   the pulse of the planets, the rhythm of tides,
   the moon makes the seasons, the day follows night,
   yet He knows every beat of my heart.
       God is great . . .

5 Let cannons of thunder salute their acclaim,
   the sunsets fly glorious banners of flame,
   the angels shout 'holy' again and again
   as they soar in the arch of the heavens.
       God is great . . .

39 He brought me to His banqueting table
(His banner over me)

Words and music: Kevin Prosch

40 He has been given

Words and music: David Fellingham

With a steady rhythm

He has been gi-ven a name a-bove all names in earth and

Hea-ven, let all cre-a-tion claim_ that Je-sus Christ is King_____

_ and Lord of all._____ He is the vic-tor o-ver

Sa-tan's reign, His blood has tri-umphed o-ver sin and shame – Je-sus

Christ is King_____ and Lord of all.

41 He has risen

Words and music: Gerald Coates,
Noel and Tricia Richards

He has__ ri - sen, He has__ ri - sen, He has__ ri - sen,

Je - sus is a - live!__ Je - sus is a - live!__

1 When the life__ flowed from His bo - dy,
2 In the grave__ God did not leave__ Him
3 If there were__ no re - sur - rec - tion

4 When the Lord rides out of Heaven,
mighty angels at His side,
they will sound the final trumpet,
from the grave we shall arise.
He has risen . . .

5 He has given life immortal—
we shall see Him face to face;
through eternity we'll praise Him,
Christ the champion of our faith.
He has risen . . .

42   Heaven's throne ascending

JESU, MEINE FREUDE   665 665 786

Words: Timothy Dudley-Smith
Music: Traditional melody,
adapted J Crüger (1598–1662)
arranged J S Bach (1685–1750)

1 Hea - ven's throne as - cend - ing, death's do - min - ion
2 Powers of dark - ness bro - ken, earth from sleep a -

end - ing, Christ the strong to save!
- wok - en, and to life re - born!

Now in glo - ry seat - ed, work on earth com -
From our na - ture's pri - son we with Christ are

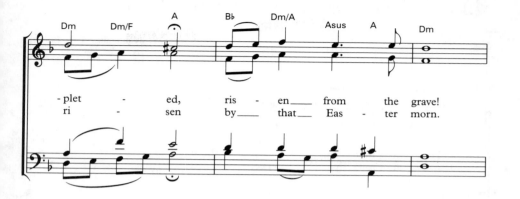

-plet - ed, ris - en___ from the grave!
ri - sen by___ that___ Eas - ter morn.

Join___ to praise through all our___ days Christ the___ Lord of___
Join___ to sing our glo - rious_ King, ris - en,___ reign - ing,___

love who_ sought___ us, and in___ dy - ing bought___ us.
high as - cend - ing, Lord of___ life_ un - end - ing!

43

Here in Your presence, Lord

Words and music: Greg Leavers

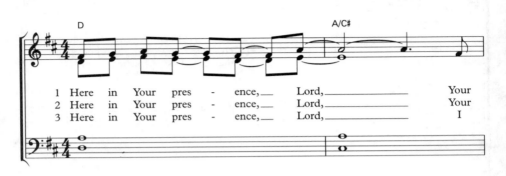

1 Here in Your pres - ence,__ Lord,_____ Your
2 Here in Your pres - ence,__ Lord,_____ Your
3 Here in Your pres - ence,__ Lord,_____ I

love is so strong,__ so____ sure.____
pow - er and love____ break____ through.__
kneel____ be - fore____ Your____ throne.__

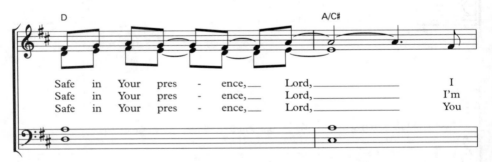

Safe in Your pres - ence,__ Lord,_____ I
Safe in Your pres - ence,__ Lord,_____ I'm
Safe in Your pres - ence,__ Lord,_____ You

rest in You so____ se - cure.____
fix - ing my eyes____ on____ You.____
tell me that I'm____ Your____ own.____ I

44 Here is bread, here is wine

Words and music: Graham Kendrick

1 Here is bread, here is wine, Christ is with us —
2 Here is grace, here is peace, Christ is with us —
3 Here we are, joined in one, Christ is with us —

He is with us; break the bread, drink the wine —
He is with us; know His grace, find His peace —
He is with us; We'll pro-claim, 'til He comes —

45 He is the Lord
(Show Your power)

Words and music: Kevin Prosch

Strong and rhythmic

1 He is___ the Lord and He reigns on high;
(2) gos - pel,___ O Lord, is the hope for our na - tion;

He is the Lord, spoke
You are the Lord. It's the

in - to___ the dark - ness, cre - a - ted___ the___ light;
pow - er___ of God for our_____ sal - va - tion;

46 Holiness is Your life in me

Words and music: Brian Doerksen

Ho-li-ness is Your life in me, mak-ing me clean through Your blood; ho-li-ness is Your fire in me, purg-ing my heart like a flood. I know You are per-fect in ho-li-ness;

com - plete; Your work of a - tone - ment

paid for__ my debts, mak-ing me ho - ly:__

on - ly the blood of Je - sus.__

Holiness is Your life in me,
making me clean through Your blood;
holiness is Your fire in me,
purging my heart like a flood.
I know You are perfect in holiness;
Your life in me, setting me free,
making me holy:
    Only the blood of Jesus
    covers all of my sin;
    only the life of Jesus
    renews me from within.
    Your blood is enough–
    Your mercy complete;
    Your work of atonement paid for my debts,
    making me holy:
    only the blood of Jesus.

47 Holy and majestic

Words and music: Julian Perkins

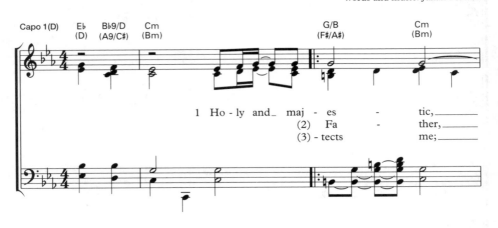

1 Ho - ly and_ maj - es - tic,_____
(2) Fa - ther,_____
(3) - tects me;_____

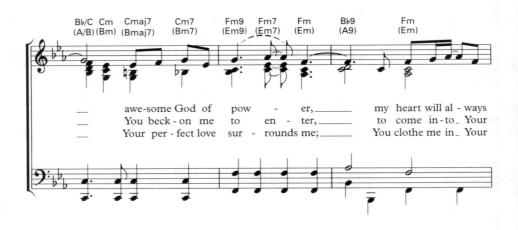

_ awe-some God of pow - er,_____ my heart will al - ways
_ You beck - on me to en - ter,_____ to come in - to_ Your
_ Your per - fect love sur - rounds me;_____ You clothe me in_ Your

praise You. Your ho - ly name I hon - our._____
pres - ence and gaze up - on_ Your glo - ry._____
beau - ty; I know Your depths of mer - cy._____

48

How can I be free from sin

Words and music: Graham Kendrick
and Steve Thompson

Moderately

mf

1 How can I___ be free from sin – lead me to the cross of
2 How can I___ know peace with-in?___ Lead me to the cross of
3 How can I___ live day by day – Lead me to the cross of

Je - sus — from the guilt, the power, the pain?
Je - sus. Sing a song of joy___ a - gain!
Je - sus, fol - low-ing___ His nar - row way?

Fine

Lead me to the cross of Je - sus.
Lead me to the cross of Je - sus.
Lead me to the cross of Je - sus.

49 How do we start
(That the world may believe)

Words and music: Chris Rolinson

1 How do we start_____ to touch the bro - ken hearts,_ the bar-ren
(2) - claim_____ the love of Je - sus Christ – a man of
(3) go_____ in - to a lone - ly world_ where fear_

lives, the lone - ly and be - reaved?_____ Lord, in Your
sor - rows, yet a man di - vine;_____ His wor - thi-
reigns and sor - row fills the air;_____ yet, as we

name_____ we shall go forth:_____ Your heal - ing
- ness,_____ His love - li - ness,_____ His faith - ful -
go_____ Your Spi - rit comes_____ Your cleans - ing

power for ev - er is the same!
- ness for ev - er we will sing!
power You give to us to share!

That the

world may be-lieve,___ that the world may be-lieve,___ that the world may be-

- lieve   in   You!_____ 2 We shall pro - ___
3 And so we

1 How do we start to touch the broken hearts,
   the barren lives, the lonely and bereaved?
   Lord, in Your name we shall go forth:
   Your healing power for ever is the same!
      That the world may believe,
      that the world may believe,
      that the world may believe in You!

2 We shall proclaim the love of Jesus Christ—
   a man of sorrows, yet a man divine;
   His worthiness, His loveliness,
   His faithfulness for ever we will sing!
      That the world may believe . . .

3 And so we go into a lonely world
   where fear reigns and sorrow fills the air;
   yet, as we go Your Spirit comes—
   Your cleansing power You give to us to share!
      That the world may believe . . .

How long, O Lord

Words: from Psalm 13
Barbara Woollett
Music: Christopher Norton

Moderately with expression

1 How long, O Lord, will You for-get an ans-wer to my prayer?__
2 How long, O Lord, will You for-sake and leave me in this way?__
3 How long, O Lord – but You for-give, with mer-cy from a-bove.__

No to-kens of Your love I see,
When will You come to my re-lief?
I find that all Your ways are just,

Your face is turned a-way from me; I wres-tle with des-
My heart is o-ver-whelmed with grief, by e-vil night and
I learn to praise You and to trust in Your un-fail-ing

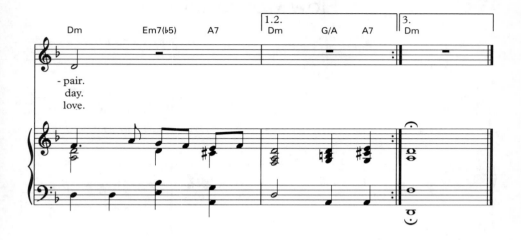

- pair.
day.
love.

1 How long, O Lord, will You forget
an answer to my prayer?
No tokens of Your love I see,
Your face is turned away from me;
I wrestle with despair.

2 How long, O Lord, will You forsake
and leave me in this way?
When will You come to my relief?
My heart is overwhelmed with grief,
by evil night and day.

3 How long, O Lord– but You forgive,
with mercy from above.
I find that all Your ways are just,
I learn to praise You and to trust
in Your unfailing love.

51 How wonderful

Words and music: Dave Bilbrough

52 I am persuaded
(We are more than conquerors)

Words and music: David J Hadden

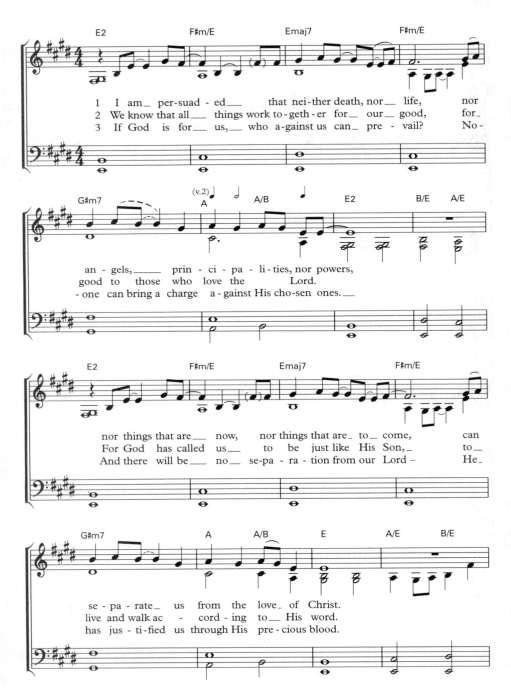

1 I am per-suad-ed that nei-ther death, nor life, nor
2 We know that all things work to-geth-er for our good, for
3 If God is for us, who a-gainst us can pre-vail? No-

an-gels, prin-ci-pa-li-ties, nor powers,
good to those who love the Lord.
-one can bring a charge a-gainst His cho-sen ones.

nor things that are now, nor things that are to come, can
For God has called us to be just like His Son, to
And there will be no se-pa-ra-tion from our Lord – He

se-pa-rate us from the love of Christ.
live and walk ac-cord-ing to His word.
has jus-ti-fied us through His pre-cious blood.

Words and music: © 1983 Restoration Music Ltd / Sovereign Music, UK,
PO Box 356, Leighton Buzzard, Beds LU7 8WP, UK.

55 I love to hear the story

THORNBURY   76 76 D

Words: E H Miller (1833–1913)
Music: Basil Harwood (1859–1949)
arranged Christopher Norton

An SATB arrangement for this tune will be found at *Combined Mission Praise* 705.

56 I should be getting to know You

Words and music: Geoff Twigg
Music arranged Richard J Hubbard

Gently, unhurried

1 I should be get-ting to know___ You: You're my Fa - ther, I'm Your
2 I should be get-ting to know___ You: for, des - pite the wrong I

child –   I should be get-ting to know___ You, the
do,   Lord, You still want me to know___ You. You

touch of Your hand,_   the warmth of Your smile._
know in my heart_   I mean to be true:_

Help me to lis - ten to Your word
teach me to love Your ho - ly ways

and then to act on what I've
and walk with-in them all my

heard;
days,

help me to know that Your love___ for me is sure___
re-main-ing loy - al to You,___ my faith-ful Friend,

—
—

O draw me clo - ser, my Fa -
be-cause I know that Your love

- ther and my Lord.
___ will ne - ver

end.

57

I sing a simple song of love
(Arms of love)

Words and music: Craig Musseau

Gently, with feeling

I sing a sim-ple song of love to my Sav - iour, to my Je - sus. I'm grate-ful for the things You've done, my lov-ing Sav-iour, O pre-cious Je - sus. My heart is glad that You've

58

I sing this song

Words and music: Ed Pirie

MEN	I sing this song
	as a simple act of worship to my Lord,
WOMEN	I sing this song
	as a simple act of worship to my Lord.
MEN	I sing this song
	as a simple act of worship to my Lord,
WOMEN	I sing this song
	as a simple act of worship to my Lord.
MEN	For He is holy,
WOMEN	holy,
MEN ·	holy,
WOMEN	holy,
ALL	holy is the Lord.
MEN	He is holy,
WOMEN	holy,
ALL	holy is the Lord.

59 I, the Lord of sea and sky
(Here I am, Lord)

From Isaiah 6
Words and music: Daniel Schutte

1 I, the Lord of sea and sky,
I have heard My peo-ple cry;
2 I, the Lord of snow and rain,
I have borne My peo-ple's pain;
3 I, the Lord of wind and flame,
I will tend the poor and lame,

all who dwell in dark and sin
My hand will save.
I have wept for love of them –
they turn a-way.
I will set a feast for them –
My hand will save.

I who made the stars of night,
I will make their dark-ness bright.
I will break their hearts of stone,
give them hearts for love a-lone;
Fin-est bread I will pro-vide
till their hearts are sa-tis-fied;

Who will bear My light to them?
Whom shall I send?_____
I will speak My word to them.
Whom shall I send?_____
I will give My life to them.
Whom shall I send?_____

60   I want to know You

Words and music: Brian Doerksen
and Cindy Rethmeier

61   I want to serve the purpose of God
(In my generation)

Words and music: Mark Altrogge

Driving

1 I want to serve the pur-pose of God in my ge-ne-ra-tion.
2 I want to build with sil-ver and gold in my ge-ne-ra-tion.
3 I want to see the king-dom of God in my ge-ne-ra-tion.
4 I want to see the Lord come a-gain in my ge-ne-ra-tion.

I want to serve the pur-pose of God while
I want to build with sil-ver and gold while
I want to see the king-dom of God while
I want to see the Lord come a-gain while

I am a-live.
I am a-live.
I am a-live.
I am a-live.

I want to give my
I want to give my
I want to give my
I want to give my

life for some-thing that-'ll last for ev-er: Oh, I de-light,

62

I will cry mercy
(Cry mercy)

Words and music: Steve Bassett
and Sue Rinaldi
Music arranged Stuart Townend

I will_ cry mer - cy, I will_ cry mer-cy for this land, O God. I will cry jus-tice, I will cry jus - tice for this land, O God, for this land, O God._____ Let Your

63   If you are encouraged

Words and music: Graham Kendrick

1 If you are en-cour-aged in your u-ni-on__ with Christ,
2 Be sure you do no-thing out of sel-fish-ness or pride,

find-ing con-so-la - tion in His love, com -
ne-ver see-ing past__ your own con-cerns, but

- pas-sion, warmth and friend-ship in the Spi-rit's flow of life;__
hum-bly keep the int - erests of each oth - er in__ your hearts,

this is how you make my joy com-plete:
see-ing them as bet - ter than your-selves: *By be-ing of the*

64 I'll go in the strength of the Lord

Words: Edward Turney
Music: Ivor Bosanko

Allegro ♩ = 120

1 I'll go in the strength of the Lord,— in paths He has marked for my
2 I'll go in the strength of the Lord,— to work He ap - points me to
3 I'll go in the strength of the Lord,— to con - flicts which faith— will re -

66 I worship You, almighty God

Words and music: Sondra Corbett

Worshipfully ♩ = 80

I wor - ship You, al - migh - ty God,_____ there is none like You. I wor - ship You, O Prince of Peace,_____ that is what I love to do. I give You praise,_____ for You are my right - eous-ness._____ I wor - ship You, al - migh - ty God,_____ there is none like You.

67   In the Lord I'll be ever thankful

Words: Taizé Community
Music: Jacques Berthier

In the Lord I'll be ev - er thank - ful, in the Lord I will re -

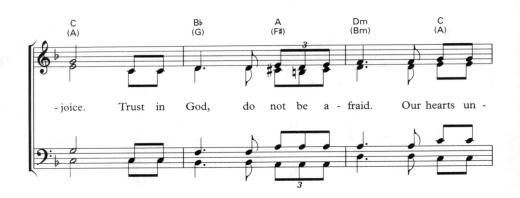

- joice. Trust in God, do not be a - fraid. Our hearts un -

Fine

- trou-bled, the Lord is near, our hearts un - trou-bled, the Lord is near. In the

68 In the streets of every city
(Where it matters, there you'll find us)

Words: Michael Perry
Music: Chris Rolinson

Forcefully

Capo 3(D)

1 In the streets of ev - ery__ ci - ty, bring-ing hope and heal - ing__
(2) world, in ev - ery__ na - tion, serv-ing Christ, with lives made
(3) dai - ly time of__ pray-ing, thank-ing God for sins for -
(4) ta - ble, there you'll find us pour-ing wine and shar - ing__
(5) ci - ty, and of__ na - tion, Lord as - cend - ed, com - ing__

strife, liv - ing out the Sav-iour's pi - ty, car - ing
whole; in His name we speak sal - va - tion grace for
- given, hear-ing what His voice is say - ing, tast-ing
bread; 'Christ has died' these gifts re - mind us, 'Christ is
King; with re - sound - ing ex - ul - ta - tion of Your

for each pre - cious life. 2 Through the
ev - ery seek - ing soul;
now the joys of Heaven. 4 At His dead'.
ri - sen from the
faith - ful - ness we sing.

1.3. 2.4.5.

Where it mat - ters, there you'll find___ us,

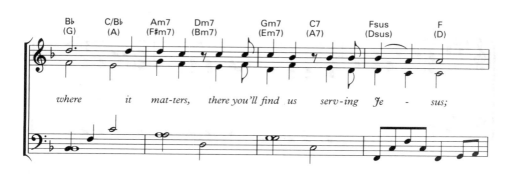

where it mat-ters, there you'll find us serv-ing Je - sus;

where it mat - ters, there you'll find us in the ser - vice of our

Lord._____

3   In our
5   God of ___

70 It is the cry of my heart
(Cry of my heart)

Words and music: Terry Butler

71

In Your arms of love

Words and music: Chris Rolinson

Slowly and tenderly

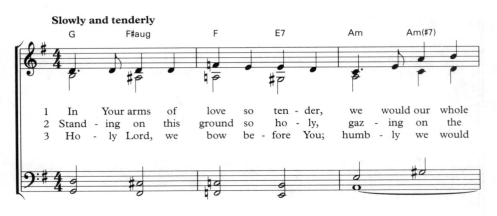

1 In Your arms of love so ten - der, we would our whole
2 Stand - ing on this ground so ho - ly, gaz - ing on the
3 Ho - ly Lord, we bow be - fore You; humb - ly we would

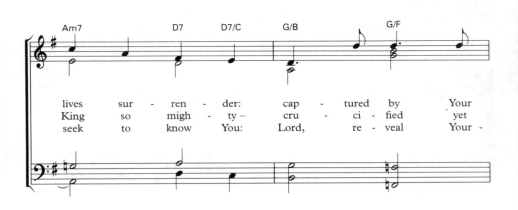

lives sur - ren - der: cap - tured by Your
King so migh - ty — cru - ci - fied yet
seek to know You: Lord, re - veal Your -

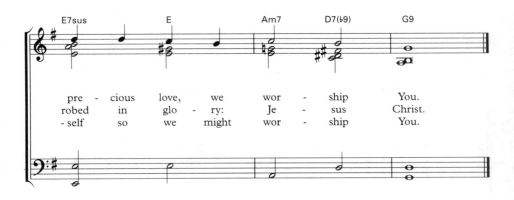

pre - cious love, we wor - ship You.
robed in glo - ry: Je - sus Christ.
- self so we might wor - ship You.

72

Jesus is the name we honour
(Jesus is our God)

Words and music: Phil Lawson Johnston

Brightly

1 Je - sus is the name we hon - our;
2 Je - sus is the name we wor - ship;
3 Je - sus is the Fa - ther's splen - dour;

Je - sus is the name we praise.
Je - sus is the name we trust.
Je - sus is the Fa - ther's joy.

Maj - es - tic name a - bove all
He is the King a - bove all
He will re - turn to reign in

we   will   lift   Him high, ___   we   will

give   Him   hon - our___ and___ praise. _____

1 Jesus is the name we honour;
   Jesus is the name we praise.
   Majestic name above all other names,
   the highest heaven and earth proclaim
        that Jesus is our God.
    We will glorify,
    we will lift Him high,
    we will give Him honour and praise.
    We will glorify . . .

2 Jesus is the name we worship;
   Jesus is the name we trust.
   He is the King above all other kings,
   let all creation stand and sing
        that Jesus is our God.
    We will glorify . . .

3 Jesus is the Father's splendour;
   Jesus is the Father's joy.
   He will return to reign in majesty,
   and every eye at last will see
        that Jesus is our God.
    We will glorify . . .

73 Jesus Christ is the Lord of all
(Lord of all)

Words and music: Gerrit Gustafson
and Steve Israel
Music arranged David Peacock

Je-sus Christ is the Lord of all, Lord of all___ the_ earth,

Je-sus Christ is the Lord of all, Lord of all___ the_ earth.

1.3.

2.4.

On - ly one God___ o - ver the na-
no oth-er name___ is there sal-va-

1.3.

- tions, on - ly one Lord_ of all;_____ in
- tion,

74 Jesus, Jesus, holy and anointed One

Words and music: John Barnett

With feeling

Je - sus, Je - sus,

ho - ly and an - oint - ed One,___ Je - sus;
ri - sen and ex - alt - ed One,___ Je -

- sus: Your name is like hon - ey on__ my lips,___ Your Spi - rit like wa-

- ter to__ my soul;___ Your word is a lamp__ un - to___ my___ feet –

___ Je - sus, I love___ You,___ I love__ You.

75 Jesus, restore to us again

Words and music: Graham Kendrick

1 Je-sus, re-
- store to us a - gain the gos - pel of Your ho - ly
name, that comes with power, not words a - lone, owned, signed and
sealed from Hea - ven's throne. Spi - rit and word in one a -

(2) Lord, e - ter - nal stands, fixed and un - chang - ing in the
heavens. The Word made flesh to earth came down to heal our
world with nail-pierced hands. A - mong us here You lived and

(3) truth, lead us, we pray, in - to all truth as we o -
- bey, and as God's will we glad - ly choose, Your an - cient
power a - gain will prove de - clare Your name — You com -

(4) heights of this dark land with Mo - ses and E - li - jah
stand: re - veal Your glo - ry once a - gain, show us Your
face, de - clare Your name — pro - phets and laws in You com -

(5) this de - ci - sive hour to know the Scrip - tures and the
power; the know-ledge in ex - per - ience prove, the power that
moves and works by love. May word and work join hands as

76 Jesus, there's no-one like You

Words and music: Alun Leppitt

Lively African style ♩ = 126

1 Je - sus,_ there's no-one like You.
2 Je - sus,_ there's no-one like You.
3 Je - sus,_ there's no-one like You.

You are the Sav-iour, You are the King, You are the
You give us life,_ You give us peace, Your pre-cious
You bring heal-ing_ and re - lease,_ so

ans-wer to ev-ery - thing._ Je - sus,_
blood has set us free._ Je - sus,_
migh-ty_ are Your deeds._ Je - sus,_

77   Jesus, take Your rightful place

Words and music: Karen David

1 Je - sus, take Your right-ful place in my life.
(2) take Your right-ful place in my heart.

I give You com-plete con - trol.
Be seat - ed on the throne.

As I lay my life a-fresh be - fore You, cleanse me and
As I lift my voice in a - do - ra - tion, I wor-ship

make me whole. You a - lone.

2 Je - sus,

78 Let the song go round the earth

MOEL LLYS 75 75 77

Words and music: S G Stock (1838–98)

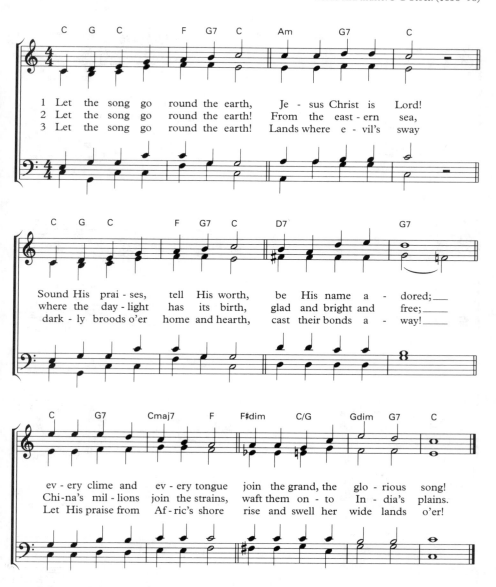

1 Let the song go round the earth,
   Jesus Christ is Lord!
   Sound His praises, tell His worth,
   be His name adored;___
   ev-ery clime and ev-ery tongue
   join the grand, the glo-rious song!

2 Let the song go round the earth!
   From the east-ern sea,
   where the day-light has its birth,
   glad and bright and free;___
   Chi-na's mil-lions join the strains,
   waft them on-to In-dia's plains.

3 Let the song go round the earth!
   Lands where e-vil's sway
   dark-ly broods o'er home and hearth,
   cast their bonds a-way!___
   Let His praise from Af-ric's shore
   rise and swell her wide lands o'er!

4 Let the song go round the earth!
   Where the summer smiles,
   let the notes of holy mirth
   break from distant isles!
   Inland forests dark and dim,
   snow-bound coasts, give back the hymn.

5 Let the song go round the earth!
   Jesus Christ is King!
   With the story of His worth
   let the whole world ring!
   Him creation all adore,
   evermore and evermore.

79

Let us draw near to God

Words and music: David Fellingham

With a steady rhythm

Let us__ draw near to God_____ in

full as - sur - ance of faith, know - ing that

as we draw near to Him, He will draw

near to us.____

Let us draw near to God
in full assurance of faith,
knowing that as we draw near to Him,
He will draw near to us.
In the Holy Place
we stand in confidence,
knowing our lives are cleansed
in the blood of the Lamb,
we will worship and adore.

80

Lord God almighty

CHRISTE SANCTORUM   11 11 11 5

Words: Timothy Dudley-Smith
Music: *Paris Antiphoner*, 1681

1 Lord God al - might - ty, Fa - ther of all mer - cies,
2 Hear us who praise_ You, first for our cre - a - tion,
3 But a - bove all___ things, for the gift of Je - sus,
4 So in thanks - giv - ing for the hope of glo - ry,

well - spring of good - ness, fount of all things liv - ing,
formed in Your like - ness, breath and be - ing gain - ing;
love past com - par - ing, source of our sal - va - tion;
love, grace and mer - cy all our days at - tend - ing,

we now Your child - ren, blessed by lov - ing kind - ness,
then for our keep - ing, life in all its ful - ness
hum - bly we bring_ You, for a world's re - deem - ing,
more than our lips,__ Lord, let our liv - ing praise_ You,

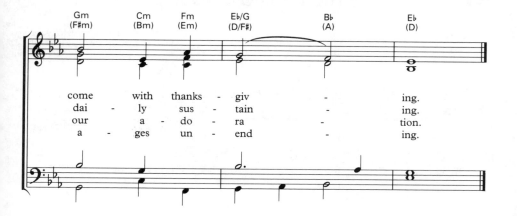

1 Lord God almighty, Father of all mercies,
   well-spring of goodness, fount of all things living,
   we now Your children, blessed by loving kindness,
   come with thanksgiving.

2 Hear us who praise You, first for our creation,
   formed in Your likeness, breath and being gaining;
   then for our keeping, life in all its fulness
   daily sustaining.

3 But above all things, for the gift of Jesus,
   love past comparing, source of our salvation;
   humbly we bring You, for a world's redeeming,
   our adoration.

4 So in thanksgiving for the hope of glory,
   love, grace and mercy all our days attending,
   more than our lips, Lord, let our living praise You,
   ages unending.

81 Lord, help me to know Your presence

Words and music: Geoff Twigg
Music arranged Richard J Hubbard

1 Lord,   help me to know_ Your pres-ence
2 Lord,   may I be-come_ like Je - sus

in all I do_ to - day, _   Lord,   help me de - clare
in ev-ery-thing I do:_   then,   if a - ny ac -

_ Your prai - ses   in ev-ery-thing I   say;_
- tion pleas - es,   glo-ry will come to You. _

82

Lord, I come to You
(The power of Your love)

Words and music: Geoff Bullock

1 Lord, I come to You,— let my heart be changed, re-newed,
2 Lord, un-veil my eyes,— let me see You face to face,—

flow-ing from the grace that I've found in
the know-ledge of Your love as You live in

You.
me.

And, Lord, I've come to know
Lord, re-new my mind,

the weak-ness-es I see in me— will be stripped a-
as Your will un-folds in my life— in liv-ing ev-ery

Lord, I lift Your name on high
(You came from Heaven to earth)

Words and music: Rick Founds

Lord, I lift Your name on high,

Lord, I love to sing Your prai - ses;

I'm so glad You're in my life,

I'm so glad You came to save us.

You came from Hea - ven to earth__ to show the way,

from the earth____ to the cross__ my debt to pay;

from the cross____ to the grave, from the grave____ to the sky,

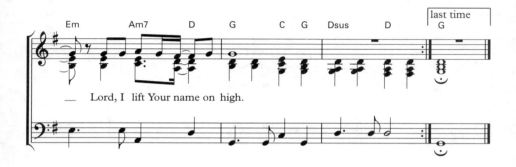

__ Lord, I lift Your name on high.

84   Lord of all hopefulness

SLANE   10 10 10 10

Words: Jan Struther (1901–53)
Music: Irish melody
arranged Christopher Norton

An SATB arrangement for this tune will be found at *Combined Mission Praise* 51.

Music arrangement: © 1993 HarperCollins*Religious* / CopyCare Ltd,
PO Box 77, Hailsham, East Sussex BN27 3EF, UK. Used by permission.

Words: from *Enlarged Songs of Praise*, 1931,
© Oxford University Press

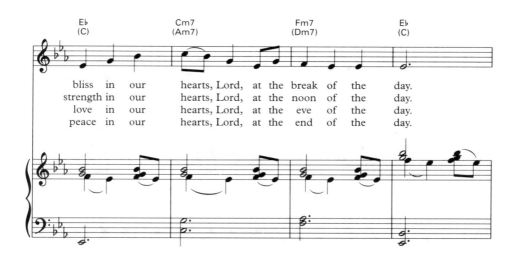

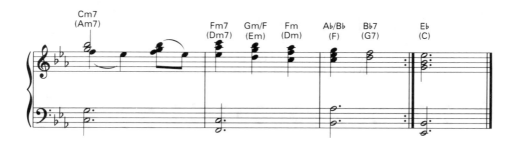

86 Lord, teach us to pray

Words and music: Geoff Twigg
Music arranged Richard J Hubbard

1 Lord, teach us to pray; let us
2 Lord, help us to see with the

know Your will ev - ery day.
eyes of faith, and be - lieve. Give us

Give us the grace to go on seek - ing Your face, in o -
Your heart to care for the world in our prayer, and a

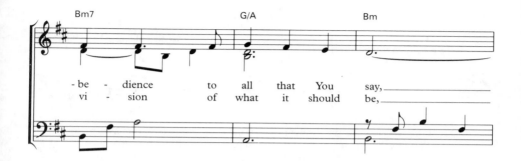

- be - dience to all that You say, _____
vi - sion of what it should be, _____

_____ in o - be - dience to all that You
_____ and a vi - sion of what it should

last time

say.
be.

1 Lord, teach us to pray;
   let us know Your will every day.
   Give us the grace
   to go on seeking Your face,
       in obedience to all that You say,
       in obedience to all that You say.

2 Lord, help us to see
   with the eyes of faith, and believe.
   Give us Your heart to care
   for the world in our prayer,
       and a vision of what it should be,
       and a vision of what it should be.

87

Lord, we come
(Go in Your name)

Words and music: Dave Bilbrough

Bright and rhythmic

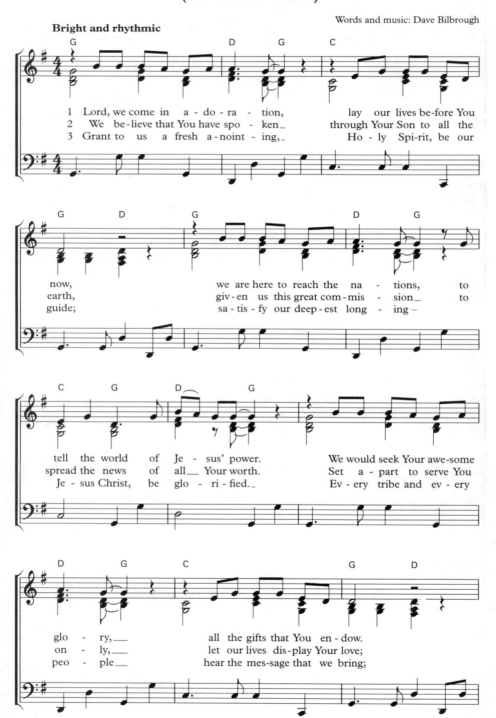

1 Lord, we come in a - do - ra - tion, lay our lives be-fore You
2 We be-lieve that You have spo - ken_ through Your Son to all the
3 Grant to us a fresh a -noint - ing,_ Ho - ly Spi-rit, be our

now, we are here to reach the na - tions, to
earth, giv-en us this great com - mis - sion_ to
guide; sa - tis - fy our deep-est long - ing —

tell the world of Je - sus' power. We would seek Your awe-some
spread the news of all_ Your worth. Set a - part to serve You
Je - sus Christ, be glo - ri - fied._ Ev - ery tribe and ev - ery

glo - ry,_ all the gifts that You en - dow.
on - ly,_ let our lives dis - play Your love;
peo - ple_ hear the mes-sage that we bring;

Called to reach this ge-ne-ra - tion,_ and now is the ap-
Hearts in-fused that tell the sto - ry___ of God come down from
Christ has tri-umphed o - ver e - vil,___ bow the knee and

-point - ed hour_ to
Heaven a - bove. go in Your name,
wor - ship Him.

go and pro-claim Your king - dom. Go___ in Your

name, for we have been cho - sen to tell all cre - a - tion that

Je - sus is King_ of all kings.

89 Lord, You have my heart

Words and music: Martin J Smith

Tenderly

Lord, You have my heart, and I will search for Yours;

Je - sus, take my life and lead me
let me be to You a sac - ri -

on.
- fice.

1.
2.

MEN And

WOMEN I will praise You,

I will praise You, Lord, and

90   Loving Shepherd of Thy sheep

BUCKLAND   77 77

Words: J E Leeson (1807–82)
Music: L G Hayne (1836–83)

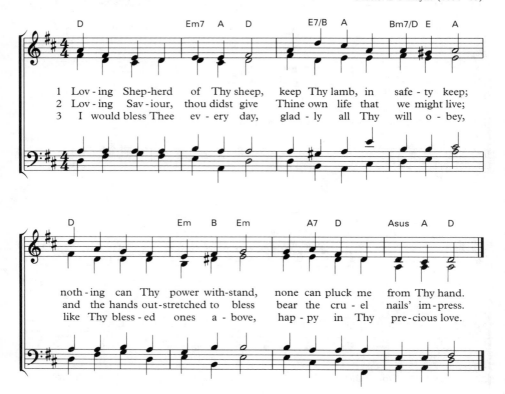

1 Lov-ing Shep-herd of Thy sheep, keep Thy lamb, in safe-ty keep;
2 Lov-ing Sav-iour, thou didst give Thine own life that we might live;
3 I would bless Thee ev-ery day, glad-ly all Thy will o-bey,

noth-ing can Thy power with-stand, none can pluck me from Thy hand.
and the hands out-stretched to bless bear the cru-el nails' im-press.
like Thy bless-ed ones a-bove, hap-py in Thy pre-cious love.

1 Loving Shepherd of Thy sheep,
   keep Thy lamb, in safety keep;
   nothing can Thy power withstand,
   none can pluck me from Thy hand.

2 Loving Saviour, thou didst give
   Thine own life that we might live;
   and the hands outstretched to bless
   bear the cruel nails' impress.

3 I would bless Thee every day,
   gladly all Thy will obey,
   like Thy blessed ones above,
   happy in Thy precious love.

4 Loving Shepherd, ever near,
   teach Thy lamb Thy voice to hear;
   suffer not my steps to stray
   from the straight and narrow way.

5 Where Thou leadest I would go,
   walking in Thy steps below,
   'til before my Father's throne
   I shall know as I am known.

91 More about Jesus

MORE ABOUT JESUS   88 88 and refrain

Words: E E Hewitt (1851–1920)
Music: J R Sweney (1837–99)

1 More a-bout Je - sus would I know; more of His grace to oth - ers show,
2 More a-bout Je - sus let me learn, more of His ho - ly will dis-cern;
3 More a-bout Je - sus, in His word hold-ing com-mun-ion with my Lord;
4 More a-bout Je - sus, on His throne, rich-es in glo-ry all His own;

more of His sav - ing ful - ness see, more of His love, who died for me.
Spi - rit of God, my tea - cher be, show-ing the things of Christ to me.
hear-ing His voice in ev - ery line, mak-ing each faith - ful say - ing mine.
more of His king-dom's sure in-crease; more of His com-ing, Prince of Peace.

More, more a-bout Je - sus, more, more a-bout Je - sus;

more of His sav - ing ful - ness see, more of His love, who died for me.

92 Mighty God

Words and music: Karen David

93   Mighty God, everlasting Father

Words and music: Mark and Helen Johnson,
Chris Bowater

In a lively half-time

Migh - ty God, ___ ev - er - last - ing Fa- - ther, won - der - ful coun - sel - lor, ___

You're the Prince of Peace. ___ 2 A

1 You are Lord of hea - ven, You are called Em - ma - nu - el; ___
light to those in dark - ness, and a guide to paths of peace;

God   is   now with us,___
love   and   mer - cy   dawns,

ev - er pres - ent   to de - li   - ver. You are God e - ter -
grace, for - give - ness and sal - va   - tion. Light for re - ve - la -

- nal,   You are Lord of all   the earth;   love has
- tion,   glo - ry to Your peo   - ple;___   Son of

come to us,_   bring - ing us_ new birth._____
the Most High,   God's love gift_ to all._____

94 More love, more power

Words and music: Jude del Hierro

Worshipfully

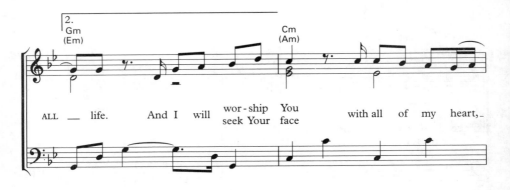

WOMEN more love, _____ more pow - er, ___

MEN More love, _____ more pow - er, _____

___ more of You ___ in my ___ life.

more of You ___ in my ___ life.

ALL ___ life. And I will wor - ship You with all of my heart, __
                        seek Your face

95 My heart is full of admiration
(All the glory)

From Psalm 45
Words and music: Graham Kendrick

96   My Jesus, I love Thee

CLARENDON STREET   11 11 11 11

Words: W R Featherstone (1846–73)
Music: A J Gordon (1836–95)

1 My Je - sus, I love___ Thee, I know Thou art
2 I love Thee be - cause.___ Thou hast first lov - èd
3 I'll love Thee in life,___ I will love Thee in
4 In man - sions of glo - ry and end - less de -

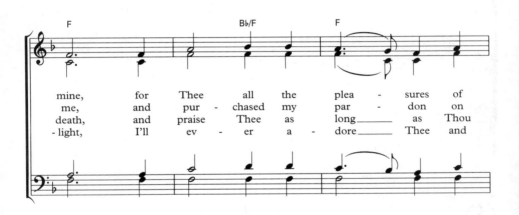

mine,   for Thee   all the plea - sures of
me,   and pur - chased my par - don on
death,   and praise Thee as long___ as Thou
- light,   I'll ev - er a - dore___ Thee and

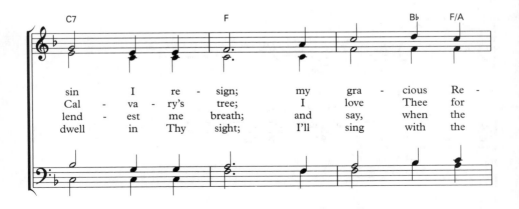

sin   I re - sign;   my gra - cious Re -
Cal - va - ry's tree;   I love Thee for
lend - est me breath;   and say, when the
dwell in Thy sight;   I'll sing with the

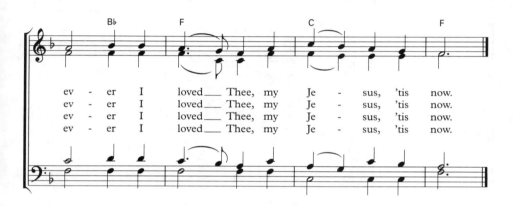

1 My Jesus, I love Thee, I know Thou art mine,
 for Thee all the pleasures of sin I resign;
 my gracious Redeemer, my Saviour art Thou,
 if ever I loved Thee, my Jesus, 'tis now.

2 I love Thee because Thou hast first lovèd me,
 and purchased my pardon on Calvary's tree;
 I love Thee for wearing the thorns on Thy brow,
 if ever I loved Thee, my Jesus, 'tis now.

3 I'll love Thee in life, I will love Thee in death,
 and praise Thee as long as Thou lendest me breath;
 and say, when the death-dew lies cold on my brow:
 if ever I loved Thee, my Jesus, 'tis now.

4 In mansions of glory and endless delight,
 I'll ever adore Thee and dwell in Thy sight;
 I'll sing with the glittering crown on my brow:
 if ever I loved Thee, my Jesus, 'tis now.

My life is in You, Lord

Words and music: Daniel Gardner

98

My lips shall praise You
(Restorer of my soul)

Words and music: Noel and Tricia Richards
arranged L Evans

My lips shall praise You, my___ great Re-deem-er; my heart will wor-ship, al-migh-ty Sav-iour.

last time **to Coda** ⊕

1 You take all my
2 Love that con-quers
3 You're the source of

guilt___ a-way, turn the dark-est night___ to___ bright-est
ev-ery fear! In the midst of trou-ble___ You draw
hap-pi-ness, bring-ing peace when I_____ am___ in___ dis-

My lips shall praise You,
my great Redeemer;
my heart will worship,
almighty Saviour.

1 You take all my guilt away,
   turn the darkest night to brightest day;
   You are the Restorer of my soul.
   My lips ...

2 Love that conquers every fear!
   In the midst of trouble You draw near,
   You are the Restorer of my soul.
   My lips ...

3 You're the source of happiness,
   bringing peace when I am in distress;
   You are the Restorer of my soul.
      My lips ...
      Almighty Saviour,
      almighty Saviour,
      almighty Saviour.

100 No other name

Words and music: Robert Gay

No oth-er name__ but the name__ of Je-sus, no oth-er

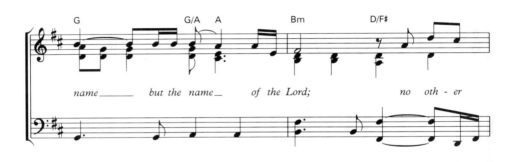

name_____ but the name__ of the Lord; no oth-er

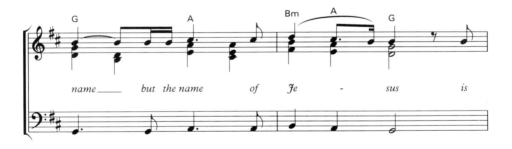

name_____ but the name of Je - sus is

last time **to Coda** ⊕

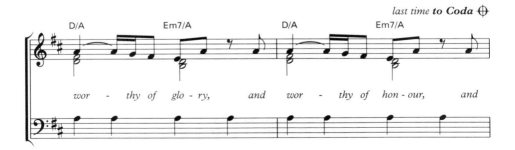

wor - thy of glo - ry, and wor - thy of hon - our, and

101 No-one but You, Lord
(Only You)

Words and music: Andy Park

Slowly, with strength

1 No - one_____ but You, Lord, can
2 Fa - ther,_____ I love You,__ come,

sat - is - fy___ the long - ing in__ my heart.__
sat - is - fy___ the long - ing in__ my heart.__

No - thing_____ I do, Lord, can
Fill me,__ o - ver - whelm me,__ un -

take the place of draw - ing near_ to You.
-til I know Your love deep in__ my heart.

On - ly

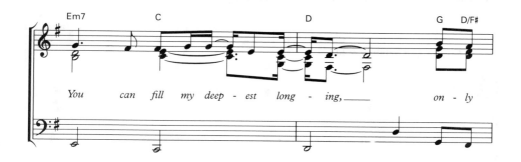

You can fill my deep - est long - ing, _____ on - ly

You can breathe in me ___ new life; _____ on - ly

You can fill my heart with laugh - ter, _____ on - ly

You can ans - wer my ___ heart's cry.

103 Now is Christ risen from the dead

LASST UNS ERFREUEN   88 44 88 with Alleluias

Words: Timothy Dudley-Smith
Music: *Geistliche Kirchengesang*
arranged David Peacock

With confidence ♩ = 148

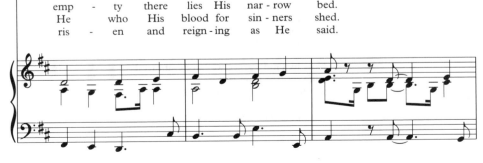

1 Now is Christ ris - en from the dead,
2 Now is Christ ris - en from the dead,
3 Now is Christ ris - en from the dead,
4 Now is Christ ris - en from the dead,

now are the powers of dark - ness fled.
emp - ty there lies His nar - row bed.
He who His blood for sin - ners shed.
ris - en and reign - ing as He said.

An alternative arrangement of this tune will be found at *Combined Mission Praise* 7.

Al – le – lu – ia, al – le – lu –

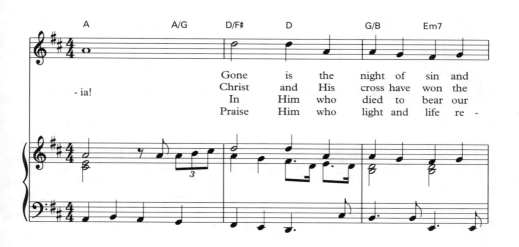

– ia!

Gone is the night of sin and
Christ and His cross have won the
In Him who died to bear our
Praise Him who light and life re –

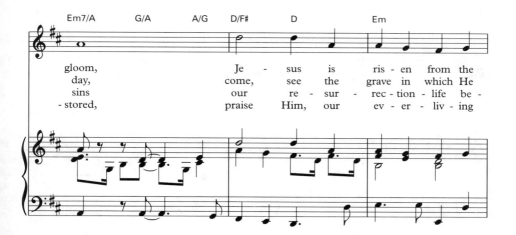

gloom, Je – sus is ris – en from the
day, come, see the grave in which He
sins our re – sur – rec – tion – life be –
– stored, praise Him, our ev – er – liv – ing

tomb.
lay.
- gins.
Lord!

Al - le - lu - ia, al - le -

- lu - ia, al - le - lu - ia, al - le -

- lu - ia, al - le - lu -

1 Now is Christ risen from the dead,
   now are the powers of darkness fled.
   Alleluia, alleluia!
   Gone is the night of sin and gloom,
   Jesus is risen from the tomb.
   Alleluia, alleluia,
   alleluia, alleluia,
   alleluia!

2 Now is Christ risen from the dead,
   empty there lies His narrow bed.
   Alleluia, alleluia!
   Christ and His cross have won the day,
   come, see the grave in which He lay.
   Alleluia, alleluia,
   alleluia, alleluia,
   alleluia!

3 Now is Christ risen from the dead,
   He who His blood for sinners shed.
   Alleluia, alleluia!
   In Him who died to bear our sins
   our resurrection-life begins.
   Alleluia, alleluia,
   alleluia, alleluia,
   alleluia!

4 Now is Christ risen from the dead,
   risen and reigning as He said.
   Alleluia, alleluia!
   Praise Him who light and life restored,
   praise Him, our ever-living Lord!
   Alleluia, alleluia,
   alleluia, alleluia,
   alleluia!

104   Now in reverence and awe

Words and music: Graham Kendrick
Music arranged Steve Thompson

Steadily

1 Now in re - ver-ence and awe___ we ga - ther round Your word;
2 Lord, Your truth can-not___ be chained; it search - es ev - ery-thing___

___ in won - der we___ draw near___ to mys - ter - ies___ that
___ my se - crets, my___ de - sires.___ Your word is like___ a

an - gels strain to hear, that
ham - mer and a fire – it

105   Now the fruit of the Spirit

Words and music: John Larsson

Now the fruit of the Spi - rit is pa - tience,

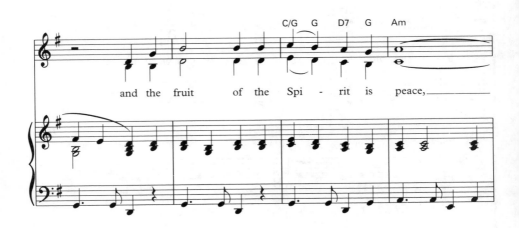

and the fruit of the Spi - rit is peace,

I am sat-is-fied___ when I find Your love.

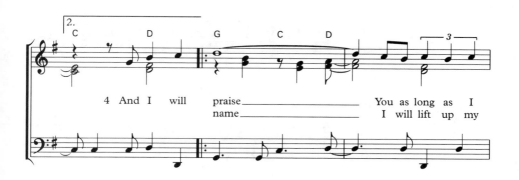

4 And I will praise_____ You as long as I
   name_____ I will lift up my

live, for Your love_____ is bet-ter than
hands, for Your love_____ is bet-ter than

life; in your
life.

107   O Christ, the King of glory

ROEWEN   76 76 D

Words: Timothy Dudley-Smith
Music: Roger Mayor

This hymn may also be sung to CRÜGER, *Combined Mission Praise* 204.

108 O Father of the fatherless
(Father me)

Words and music: Graham Kendrick

1 O Fa - ther of___ the fa - ther-less___ in whom all fa - mi -
(2) bruised and bro - ken I draw near, You hold me close and
(3) in my fool - ish-ness I stray, re - turn - ing emp - ty
(4) when I look___ in - to Your eyes, from deep with - in my

- lies are blessed, I love____ the way You fa - ther me.____
dry my tears, I love____ the way You fa - ther me.____
and a - shamed, I love____ the way You fa - ther me.____
spi - rit cries: I love____ the way You fa - ther me.____

You gave me life, for - gave the past; now in Your arms I'm
At last my fear - ful heart is still,_ sur - rend-ered to Your
Ex - chang-ing for_ my wretch-ed-ness Your rad - iant robes of
Be - fore such love I stand a - mazed, and ev - er will through

109 O God of Bethel

BURFORD CM

Words: P Doddridge (1702–51)
and J Logan (1748–88)
Music: *Chetham's Psalmody*, 1718

1 O God of Bethel, by whose hand Thy people still are fed, who through this weary pilgrim-

2 Our vows, our prayers, we now pre - sent before Thy throne of grace; God of our fa - thers, be the

3 Through each per - plex - ing path of life our wan - dering foot - steps guide; give us each day our dai - ly

4 O spread Thy cov - ering wings a - round, 'til all our wan - derings cease, and at our Fa - ther's loved a -

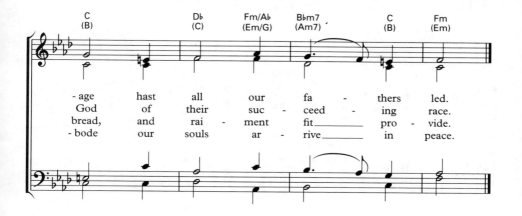

- age   hast   all   our   fa - thers   led.
God   of   their   suc - ceed - ing   race.
bread,   and   rai - ment   fit___ pro - vide.
- bode   our   souls   ar - rive___ in   peace.

1 O God of Bethel, by whose hand
    Thy people still are fed,
    who through this weary pilgrimage
    hast all our fathers led.

2 Our vows, our prayers, we now present
    before Thy throne of grace;
    God of our fathers, be the God
    of their succeeding race.

3 Through each perplexing path of life
    our wandering footsteps guide;
    give us each day our daily bread,
    and raiment fit provide.

4 O spread Thy covering wings around,
    'til all our wanderings cease,
    and at our Father's loved abode
    our souls arrive in peace.

110   O Lord, hear my prayer

Words: from Psalm 130
Music: Jacques Berthier

Recorder duo

Desc.

Treble

Flute duo

1

2

legato

Oboe

Bb Clarinet

111   O Lord, the refuge

O LORD, THE REFUGE   11 10 11 10

Words: from Psalm 90
Basil E Bridge
Music: Christopher Norton

1 O Lord, the re-fuge of each ge-ne-ra-tion, You
(2) thou - sand years like yes-ter - day in pass-ing, our
(3) Ho - ly Lord, for-give our self - de-ceiv-ing our
(4) rush - es on: give us a heart of wis - dom that

reigned be - fore the u - ni - verse be - gan; we bear Your
fleet - ing lives like half - re - mem-bered dreams, or weeds that
se - cret sins are clear be - fore Your face: grant us re -
seeks Your will and fol - lows Your com-mands; show us Your

stamp, the marks of Your cre - a - tion, and yet how
flower at noon but die by eve - ning - so, Lord, to
- lease, the joy of those be - liev-ing they are re -
deeds, Your glo - ry to our child - ren, work out Your

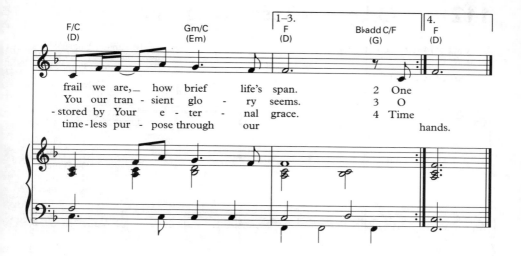

1 O Lord, the refuge of each generation,
  You reigned before the universe began;
  we bear Your stamp, the marks of Your creation,
  and yet how frail we are, how brief life's span.

2 One thousand years like yesterday in passing,
  our fleeting lives like half-remembered dreams,
  or weeds that flower at noon but die by evening–
  so, Lord, to You our transient glory seems.

3 O Holy Lord, forgive our self-deceiving–
  our secret sins are clear before Your face:
  grant us release, the joy of those believing
  they are restored by Your eternal grace.

4 Time rushes on: give us a heart of wisdom
  that seeks Your will and follows Your commands;
  show us Your deeds, Your glory to our children,
  work out Your timeless purpose through our hands.

112 O Lord, whose saving name

DARWALL'S 148TH   66 66 44 44

Words: Timothy Dudley-Smith
Music: John Darwall (1731–89)
arranged Roger Mayor

1 O Lord, whose sav-ing name is life and health and rest, to whom the child-ren came and in Your
2 That love be ours to share with ten-der-ness and skill, with sci-ence, faith and prayer to work Your
3 When deep-est sha-dows fall to quench life's fad-ing spark, be near us when we call, walk with us
4 In God our hope is set, be-neath whose rule a-lone is peace from fear and fret and strength be-
5 Join ev-ery heart to bring our praise to God a-bove, whom child-ren's voi-ces sing and whom un-

An SATB arrangement of this tune will be found at *Combined Mission Praise* 783.

Music arrangement: © Roger Mayor / Jubilate Hymns

113

O spread the tidings
(The Comforter has come)

COMFORTER   12 12 12 6 and refrain

Words: F Bottome (1823–94)
Music: W J Kirkpatrick (1838–1921)

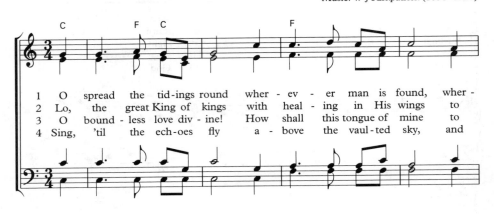

1 O spread the tid-ings round wher - ev - er man is found, wher -
2 Lo, the great King of kings with heal - ing in His wings to
3 O bound - less love div - ine! How shall this tongue of mine to
4 Sing, 'til the ech-oes fly a - bove the vaul - ted sky, and

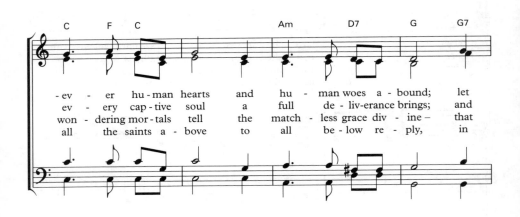

- ev - er hu - man hearts and hu - man woes a - bound; let
ev - ery cap - tive soul a full de - liv-erance brings; and
won - dering mor - tals tell the match - less grace div - ine – that
all the saints a - bove to all be - low re - ply, in

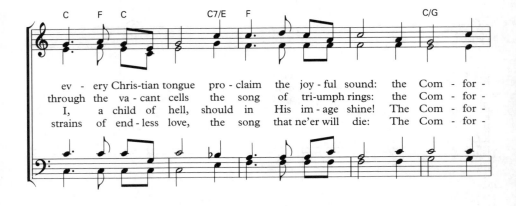

ev - ery Chris-tian tongue pro - claim the joy - ful sound: the Com - for -
through the va - cant cells the song of tri-umph rings: the Com - for -
I, a child of hell, should in His im - age shine! The Com - for -
strains of end - less love, the song that ne'er will die: The Com - for -

114   Oh, I was made for this

Words and music: Graham Kendrick

1 Oh, I was made for this: to know Your ten-der kiss, to know a
2 My feet were made to dance, my spi-rit made to soar, my life is
3 When I was far a-way You ran to wel-come me, I felt Your

love div-ine, to know this love is mine. And I was
not by chance, You give me more and more. For I was
warm em-brace; I saw Your smi-ling face. And when You

made to laugh, and I was made to sing, giv-en the gift of life: You gave me
made for You, and I have made my choice, and all that stole my joy, I left it
res-cued me I saw my des-ti-ny: to wor-ship You, my Lord, to be a

1.
ev-ery - thing. ___

2.3.
at the cross. ___
friend of God. ___

So I will ce - le - brate and drink Your cup of joy, I will give

thanks each day___ and sing.___ My joy is found in You and You are

all my joy, oh, I was made_____ for this.

I was made to love You, Je - sus, I was

made for this. made for this.

115 One thing I ask

From Psalm 84
Words and music: Andy Park

1 One thing I ask, one thing I
2 Hear me, O Lord, hear me when I

seek, that I may dwell in Your
cry; Lord, do not hide Your

house, O Lord, all of my
face from me: You have been my

days, all of my life –
strength, You have been my shield,

that I may see You, Lord.
and You will lift me

up.   One__ thing   I

ask, one thing I de - sire is to see You,__

is to see You.__

116

Only by grace

Words and music: Gerrit Gustafson

Gently

On - ly by grace can we en - ter,

on - ly by grace can we stand; not by our hu - man en - dea-

- vour, but by the blood of the Lamb.

In - to Your pres - ence You call us, You call us to come;

in - to Your pres - ence You draw us, and

117   Open our eyes, O Lord

BISHOPTHORPE   CM

Words: Timothy Dudley-Smith
Music: J Clarke (c1674–1707)

1 O - pen___ our eyes,___ O Lord,___ we pray,___ en -
2 O - pen___ our ears,___ that, small___ and still,___ Your
3 O - pen___ our lives___ to love's___ em - brace,___ our
4 O - pen___ our lips,___ O Lord,___ in praise___ to

- light - en heart___ and mind;___ that as___ we read Your
voice___ be clear - ly heard, to guide___ our steps and
dear___ re - deem - ing Lord:___ Your word___ of life and
tell___ what love im - parts:___ the work___ of grace a -

word___ to - day we___ may___ its trea - sures find.
cleanse our will ac - cord - ing to___ Your word.
truth___ and grace with - in___ our souls___ be stored.
- bout___ our ways, your___ word___ with - in___ our hearts.

118 Out of a heart of love
(All-embracing love)

Words: Phil Thompson
Music: Paul Field

1 Out of a heart of love____
2 You move in signs and won - ders,

You gave cre - a - tion birth;____
fill hea - ven with Your praise, ____

with grace and pow - er and might, ____ You formed a
and in Your mer - cy hold____ all things with -

per - fect earth.
- in Your gaze. ____

Such a migh - ty God,
I am a - mazed, O Fa -

119 Our dear Father
(The Lord's prayer)

Words: from Matthew 6
Music: Lawson Spiller
arranged Julian Perkins

Our dear Fa - ther_ who art in Hea- -ven, hal-low-èd be Your name, Your king-dom come, Your will be done_ on earth as it is in Hea - ven. Give us this day_ our dai - ly bread, _ and for-

120   Overwhelmed by love

Words and music: Noel Richards

With feeling

1 O - ver - whelmed by love,
2 All my sin was laid

deep - er than o - ceans, high as the hea - vens;
on Your dear Son,____ Your prec - ious one.____

ev - er - liv - ing God,
All my debt He paid –

Your love has res - cued me.
great is Your love for me.

No - one could ev - - - er earn Your

love, Your grace and mer - cy is free. _____

Lord, these words are true —

so is my love for You.

121 Part the waters that surround me
(You're the holy Lord almighty)

Words and music: Rick Cole

Part the wa - ters that sur - round me,

may the wind and waves be still.

Pierce the soul of my con - fu - sion, clear the mist

122   Praise the Lord, you heavens

AUSTRIA   87 87 D

Words: from Psalm 148
vv. 1–2 *Foundling Hospital Collection* (1796)
v. 3 E Osler (1798–1863)
Music: Croatian folk tune
arranged Christopher Norton

1 Praise the Lord, you heavens, a - dore Him – praise Him, an - gels
2 Praise the Lord, for He is glo - rious! Ne - ver shall His
3 Wor - ship, hon - our, glo - ry, bless - ing, Lord, we of - fer

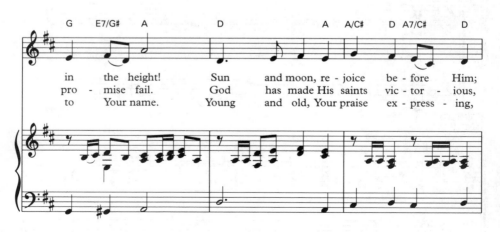

in the height! Sun and moon, re - joice be - fore Him;
pro - mise fail. God has made His saints vic - tor - ious;
to Your name. Young and old, Your praise ex - press - ing,

An SATB arrangement of this tune will be found at *Combined Mission Praise 173.*

Music arrangement: © 1993 HarperCollins*Religious* / CopyCare Ltd,
PO Box 77, Hailsham, East Sussex BN27 3EF, UK. Used by permission.

123 Purify my heart

Words and music: Brian Doerksen

Prayerfully

1 Pur - i - fy__ my heart, let me be as gold and__
2 Pur - i - fy__ my heart, cleanse me from with - in and__

pre - cious sil - ver; pur - i - fy__ my heart,__ let me be as
make me ho - ly; pur - i - fy__ my heart,__ cleanse me from my

gold, pure__ gold. Re - fin - er's fire,
sin, deep with - in.

__ my heart's one de - sire__

124   Rumours of angels

Words and music: Graham Kendrick

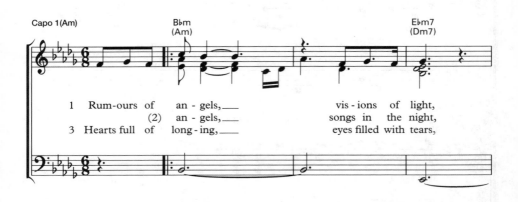

1 Rum-ours of an - gels, ___ vis - ions of light,
(2) an - gels, ___ songs in the night,
3 Hearts full of long - ing, ___ eyes filled with tears,

new star ap - pear-ing, ___ pierc - ing the night.
deep in the dan - ger, ___ un - quench-ab - le light.
na-tions are wait-ing ___ at the end of the years.

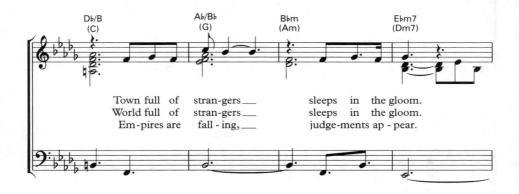

Town full of stran-gers ___ sleeps in the gloom.
World full of stran-gers ___ sleeps in the gloom.
Em-pires are fall - ing, ___ judge-ments ap - pear.

125

See how the world groans
(Here am I, my Lord)

Words and music: Howard Davies

WOMEN 1 See how the world groans be-neath sin's spell!
MEN 2 How can I go with my sin and shame?
ALL 3 Make me a ser - vant to serve just You —

Lord, who will go? Lord, who will go?
Great God on high! Lord, who am I?
Lord, I'll o-bey, use me, I pray!

*Altos each verse

ALL Some - one must care for them, some - one tell, tell of
ALL Cleanse now my heart with the liv - ing flame! Make me
ALL Teach me to speak — may my life ring true! All my

Christ, tell of His power to set men free!_____
pure, O make me strong – Lord, I will go._____
words and all my ac - tions pleas-ing You!_____

Here am

I, my Lord! Send me, send me! *I am want - ing to*

*Men stay on melody
**Add soprano – last chorus

126   Salvation belongs to our God

Words and music: Adrian Howard
and Pat Turner

1 Sal - va - tion be - longs to our God, who
(2) we, the re - deemed, shall be strong in

sits on the throne, and un - to the
pur - pose and u - ni - ty, de - clar - ing a -

Lamb. Praise and glo - ry, wis - dom and thanks,
- loud: praise and glo - ry, wis - dom and thanks,

hon - our and pow - er and strength
hon - our and pow - er and strength be to our God for

Words and music: © 1985 Restoration Music Ltd / Sovereign Music UK,
PO Box 356, Leighton Buzzard, Beds LU7 8WP, UK.

ev - er___ and ev - er, be to our God for

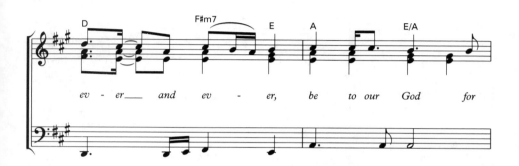

ev - er___ and ev - er, be to our God for

ev - er___ and ev - er, a - men.

2 And

127 See His glory

Words and music: Chris Bowater

128   Shalom, shalom

Words and music: Elaine Davis

With a quiet intensity

Sha-lom, sha-lom, _ peace to His peo - ple;

sham-lom, sha-lom, _ the grace of God be _ with

you, now and for ev - er! _

1 The love_ of God be_ with_ you,____
2 The grace_ of God be_ with_ you,____
3 The peace of God be_ with_ you,____

129

Shout for joy and sing

Words and music: David Fellingham

Bright, with a Latin rhythm

Shout for joy and sing your prai-ses to the King; _ lift your voice and let your hal-le-lu-jahs ring. _ Come be-fore His throne to wor-ship and a-dore; _ en-ter joy-ful-ly now _ the pre-sence of the Lord. _ You are my Cre-

130 Since the day the angel came

(Thorns in the straw)

Words and music: Graham Kendrick

1 Since the day the angel came it seemed that
(2) blan - ket on the floor of a
(3) words of an - cient seers tum - bled

ev - ery-thing had changed. The on - ly cer-tain thing was the
va - cant cat - tle - stall, but there the child was born. She
down the cen - tu - ries – a vir - gin shall con - ceive, God

child that moved with-in on the road that would not end, wind - ing
held Him in her arms and as she laid Him down to sleep, she won-dered,
with us, Prince of Peace. Man of sor - rows – stran - gest name. Oh Jo - seph,

4 And as she watched Him through the years,
  her joy was mingled with her tears,
  and she'd feel it all again,
  the glory and the shame.
  And when the miracles began,
  she wondered, 'Who is this man,
  and where will this all end?'

5 'Til, against a darkening sky,
  the one she loved was lifted high,
  and with His dying breath
  she heard Him say, 'Father, forgive!'
  and to the criminal beside,
  'Today– with me, in Paradise.'
  So bitter, yet so sweet.
  And did she see . . .

131 Sing to the Lord a joyful song

ANTWERP   LM

Words: William Smallwood (1831–97)
Music: J S B Monsell (1811–75)

1 Sing to the Lord a joyful song, lift up your hearts, your voices raise; to us His gracious gifts belong, to Him our songs of love and praise.

2 For life and love, for rest and food, for daily help and nightly care, sing to the Lord, for He is good, and praise His name, for it is fair.

3 For strength to those who on Him wait His truth to prove, His will to do, praise ye our God, for He is great, trust in His name, for it is true.

4 For joys untold, that from above
  cheer those who love His sweet employ,
  sing to our God, for He is love,
  exalt His name, for it is joy.

5 Sing to the Lord of Heaven and earth,
  whom angels serve and saints adore,
  the Father, Son and Holy Ghost,
  to whom be praise for evermore.

132 Sing a song of celebration
(We will dance)

Words and music: David Ruis

With strength

1 Sing a song of cel-e-bra-tion, lift up a
2 Dance with all your might, lift up your hands and

shout of praise, for the Bride-groom will come,
clap for joy; the time's draw-ing near

the glo-ri-ous One,
when He will ap-pear,

and oh, we will look on His
and oh, we will stand by His

face,_____ we'll go_____

side,_____ a strong,_____

_____ to a much bet-ter place._____

pure, spot-less bride._____ *Oh,*

we will dance on the streets that are__ gol-den, the glo-ri-ous

133 So many centuries
(Nothing will ever be the same)

Words and music: Graham Kendrick

1 So many cen - tu-ries of watch-ing and wait - ing,
2 In all the clam - our just a new ba - by cry - ing,
3 So rare we re - cog-nize our his-tory in the mak - ing,
4 And now a door is stand-ing o - pen be-fore you,

but when the mo-ment came, well, no - bo - dy saw,
one more poor fa - mi - ly shut out in the cold.
meet an - gels un - a - wares and pass on our way,
cast - ing its light in - to the dark - ness a - round;

tra - ders and tra - vel - lers hur - ried by,
No - thing un - us - u - al, sad to say –
blind to the mo - ment of des - ti - ny,
stop for a mo - ment, step in - side,

and life went on just like be - fore,
has - n't it al - ways been this way?
while pre - cious years just slip a - way,
to-night could be your Beth - le - hem.

since the night_____ He   came._____
since the night_____ He

_   And   came._____

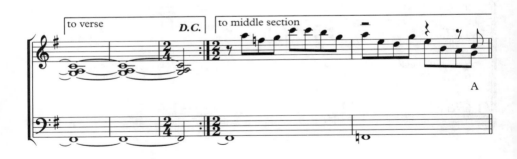

child____ is   born,__   a   Son____ is given,__   and His

king - dom of peace___ will ne - ver end. A

child___ is born,___ a Son___ is given,___ and His

king - dom of peace___ will ne - ver end, ne - ver end, no!

And

134 Standing on the promises

STANDING ON THE PROMISES   11 11 11 9 and refrain

Words and music:
R K Carter (1849–1928)

1 Stand - ing on the pro - mis - es of Christ my King,
2 Stand - ing on the pro - mis - es that can - not fail,
3 Stand - ing on the pro - mis - es I now can see

through e - ter - nal a - ges let His prai - ses ring:
when the howl - ing storms of doubt and fear as - sail
per - fect, pres - ent cleans - ing in the blood for me;

'Glo - ry in the high - est!' I will shout and sing,
by the liv - ing word of God I shall pre - vail,
stand - ing in the li - ber - ty where Christ makes free,

stand - ing on the pro - mis - es of God.
stand - ing on the pro - mis - es of God.
stand - ing on the pro - mis - es of God.

Stand - ing,
Stand - ing on the pro - mise,

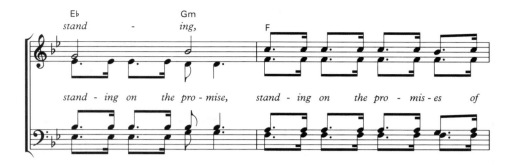

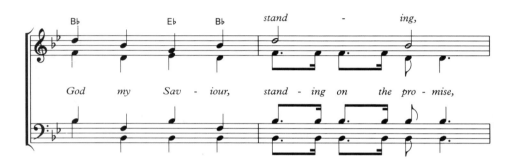

4 Standing on the promises of Christ the Lord,
bound to Him eternally by love's strong cord,
overcoming daily with the Spirit's sword,
standing on the promises of God.
Standing, standing . . .

5 Standing on the promises I cannot fall,
listening every moment to the Spirit's call,
resting in my Saviour as my all in all,
standing on the promises of God.
Standing, standing . . .

136 Sweet feast of love divine

FRANCONIA SM

Words: E Denny (1796–1889)
Music: *Harmonischer Liederschatz*, 1738

1 Sweet feast of love di - vine! 'Tis
2 Here ev - ery wel - come guest waits,
3 Here con - science ends its strife, and

grace that makes us free to feed up - on this
Lord, from Thee to learn the sec - rets of Thy
faith de - lights to prove the sweet - ness of the

bread and wine in mem - ory, Lord, of Thee.
Fa - ther's breast, and all Thy grace dis - cern.
bread of life, the ful - ness of Thy love.

4 Thy blood that flowed for sin,
   in symbol here we see,
   and feel the blessed pledge within,
   that we are loved of Thee.

5 But if this glimpse of love
   is so divinely sweet,
   what will it be, O Lord, above,
   Thy gladdening smile to meet;

6 To see Thee face to face,
   Thy perfect likeness wear,
   and all Thy ways of wondrous grace
   Through endless years declare!

137 Take up your cross

Breslau   LM

Words: from Mark 8
C W Everest (1814–77)
Music: *Hymnodus Sacer,* 1625
arranged F Mendelssohn (1809–47)

1 'Take up your cross!' the Sav - iour___ said, 'if
2 Take up your cross – let not its___ weight fill
3 Take up your cross, nor heed the___ shame, nor

you would my dis - ci - ple___ be; de - ny your - self, the
your weak spi - rit___ with a - larm: His___ strength shall___ bear your
let your fool - ish___ pride re - bel: your___ Lord for___ you the

world for - sake and hum - bly fol - low___ af - ter___ me.'
spi - rit___ up, and brace your heart, and___ nerve your___ arm.
cross___ en - dured to save your soul___ from___ death and___ hell.

4 Take up your cross, then, in His strength,
  and calmly every danger brave;
  'twill guide you to a better home,
  and lead to victory o'er the grave.

5 Take up your cross, and follow Christ,
  nor think 'til death to lay it down;
  for only he who bears the cross
  may hope to wear the glorious crown.

6 To You, great Lord, the One-in-three,
  all praise for evermore ascend:
  O grant us in our home to see
  the heavenly life that knows no end.

138   Teach me to dance

Words and music: Graham Kendrick
and Steve Thompson

Teach me to dance to the beat of Your heart,____ teach me to move
with Your heart of com-pas - sion, teach me to trust

in the power of Your Spi - rit, teach me to walk in the light of Your pres-
in the word of Your pro - mise, teach me to hope in the day of Your com-

last time **to Coda** ⊕

- ence, teach me to dance to the beat of Your heart. _ Teach me to love
- ing, teach me to dance to the beat of Your heart.

1 You wrote the rhy - thm of life,
2 Let all my move-ments ex - press

139

Thank You for saving me

Words and music: Martin J Smith

1 Thank You for sav - ing me; what can I say?
2 Mer - cy and grace are mine – for - given is my sin.

You are my ev - ery-thing, I will sing Your praise.
Je - sus, my on - ly hope, the Sav-iour of the world.

You shed Your blood for me; what can I say?
'Great is the Lord', we cry, 'God, let Your king-dom come!'

You took my sin and shame, a sin-ner called by name.
Your word has let me see, thank You for sav - ing me.

140   The crucible for silver

Words and music: Martin J Smith
arranged D J Langford

1 The cru - ci - ble__ for sil - ver __ and the
2 Fa - ther, take__ our off - ering, __ with our

fur - nace__ for gold,__ but the Lord tests the heart of this child.
song we humb-ly praise You. You have brought Your ho-ly fire to our lips.

Stand-ing in__ all pu - ri - ty, God, our pas-sion is__ for ho - li-ness;
Stand-ing in__ Your beau - ty, Lord, Your__ gift to us__ is ho - li-ness;

141

The Lord is exalted
(The day of His power)

Words and music: Steve Chua
and Ed Pirie

1 The Lord is ex-alt - ed___ at God's right hand,
2 He's raised up an ar - my,___ the weak and the lost. __

His ban-ner un-furl - ing___
He's called us to fol - low,___

a-cross the__ land. __
ac-cept-ing the cost, __

All power and do - min -
and if we are faith-

- ion___
- ful___

shall kneel at His throne,
and trust His com-mands,

142   The love of God comes close

RHOSYMEDRE   66 66 888

Words: John L Bell and Graham Maule
Music: John David Edwards (1805–85)

1 The love of God comes close where stands an o - pen door
2 The peace of God comes close to those caught in the storm,
3 The joy of God comes close where faith en - coun - ters fears,

to let the stran - ger in, to min - gle rich and poor.
for - go - ing lives of ease to ease the lives for - lorn.
where heights and depths of life are found through smiles and tears.

The love of God is here to stay; em - brac - ing those who
The peace of God is here to stay; em - brac - ing those who
The joy of God is here to stay; em - brac - ing those who

From the *Enemy of Apathy* collection, (Wild Goose Publications 1988) by John L Bell and Graham Maule

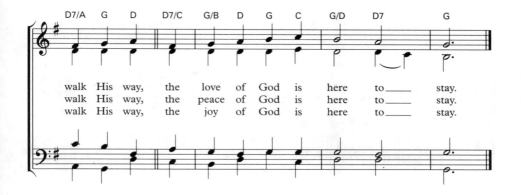

walk His way, the love of God is here to_____ stay.
walk His way, the peace of God is here to_____ stay.
walk His way, the joy of God is here to_____ stay.

1 The love of God comes close
          where stands an open door
     to let the stranger in,
              to mingle rich and poor.
     The love of God is here to stay;
     embracing those who walk His way,
     the love of God is here to stay.

2 The peace of God comes close
              to those caught in the storm,
     forgoing lives of ease
              to ease the lives forlorn.
     The peace of God is here to stay;
     embracing those who walk His way,
     the peace of God is here to stay.

3 The joy of God comes close
          where faith encounters fears,
     where heights and depths of life
              are found through smiles and tears.
     The joy of God is here to stay;
     embracing those who walk His way,
     the joy of God is here to stay.

4 The grace of God comes close
              to those whose grace is spent,
     when hearts are tired or sore
              and hope is bruised and bent.
     The grace of God is here to stay;
     embracing those who walk His way,
     the grace of God is here to stay.

5 The Son of God comes close
          where people praise His name,
     where bread and wine are blessed
              and shared as when He came.
     The Son of God is here to stay;
     embracing those who walk His way,
     the Son of God is here to stay.

143   The precious blood of Jesus

Words and music: John Barnett

The pre - cious blood of Je - sus,___ the
pre - cious name of Je - sus,___ the

on - ly cleans-ing___ power___ my guilt___ and shame are
name___ by which we're_ saved.___ He bore___ the cross I

washed a - way_ be-neath its crim - son_ flood. The
should have had,_ a

144 There is a place of quiet rest
(Near to the heart of God)

NEAR TO THE HEART OF GOD   CM and refrain

Words and music: C B McAfee
(1866–1944)

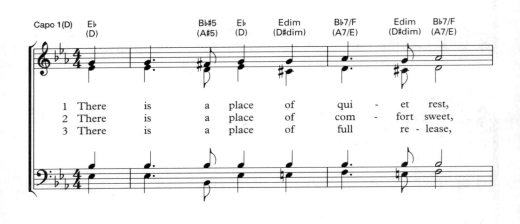

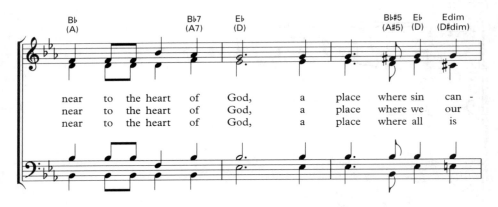

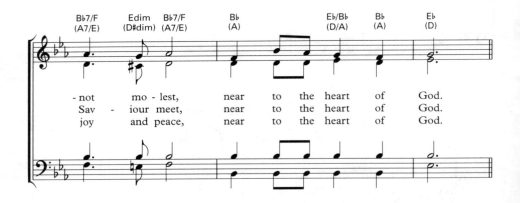

1 There is a place of qui - et rest,
2 There is a place of com - fort sweet,
3 There is a place of full re - lease,

near to the heart of God, a place where sin can -
near to the heart of God, a place where we our
near to the heart of God, a place where all is

- not mo - lest, near to the heart of God.
Sav - iour meet, near to the heart of God.
joy and peace, near to the heart of God.

1 There is a place of quiet rest,
  near to the heart of God,
  a place where sin cannot molest,
  near to the heart of God.
  O Jesus, blest Redeemer,
  sent from the heart of God,
  hold us who wait before Thee
  near to the heart of God.

2 There is a place of comfort sweet,
  near to the heart of God,
  a place where we our Saviour meet,
  near to the heart of God.
  O Jesus . . .

3 There is a place of full release,
  near to the heart of God,
  a place where all is joy and peace,
  near to the heart of God.
  O Jesus . . .

145 There is none like You

Words and music: Lenny LeBlanc

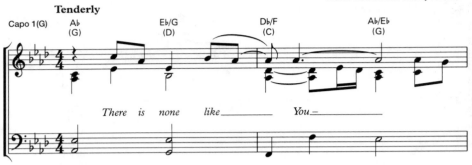

Tenderly

There is none like You—

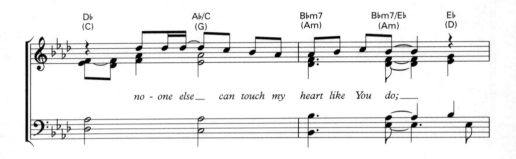

no - one else— can touch my heart like You do;—

I could search for all e - ter - ni - ty long— and find

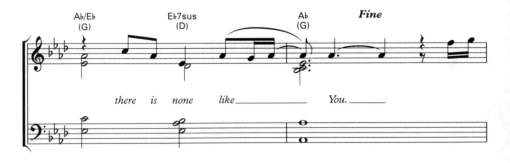

there is none like You.

146 There is power in the name of Jesus

Words and music: Noel Richards

Rocky

1 There is power— in the name of Je - sus;
(2) — in the name of Je - sus,

we be - lieve— in His name.
like a sword— in our hands.

We have called on the name of Je - sus;
We de - clare,— in the name of Je - sus,

we are saved, we are saved!
we shall stand, we shall stand.

147   There shall be showers of blessing

SHOWERS OF BLESSING   87 87 and refrain

Words: El Nathan (1840–1901)
Music: J McGranahan (1840–1907)

Not too fast

Capo 3(G)

1 'There shall be show - ers of bless - ing':_____
2 'There shall be show - ers of bless - ing':_____
3 'There shall be show - ers of bless - ing':_____

this is the pro - mise of love; there shall be sea - sons re -
pre - cious re - viv - ing a - gain; o - ver the seas and the
send them up - on us, O Lord! Grant to us now a re -

- fresh - ing, sent from the Sav - iour a - bove.
val - leys, sound of a - bun - dance of rain.
- fresh - ing; come, and now hon - our Thy word.

Show - *ers* *of* *bless* - *ing,*
Show - *ers,* *show* - *ers*

show - ers of bless - ing we need, mer - cy drops round us are

fall - ing, _____ but for the show - ers we plead.

1 'There shall be showers of blessing':
  this is the promise of love;
  there shall be seasons refreshing,
  sent from the Saviour above.
    Showers of blessing,
    showers of blessing we need,
    mercy drops round us are falling,
    but for the showers we plead.

2 'There shall be showers of blessing':
  precious reviving again;
  over the seas and the valleys,
  sound of abundance of rain.
    Showers of blessing . . .

3 'There shall be showers of blessing':
  send them upon us, O Lord!
  Grant to us now a refreshing;
  come, and now honour Thy word.
    Showers of blessing . . .

4 'There shall be showers of blessing':
  Oh, that today they might fall,
  now, as to God we're confessing,
  now, as to Jesus we call.
    Showers of blessing . . .

5 'There shall be showers of blessing':
  if we but trust and obey;
  there shall be seasons refreshing,
  if we let God have His way.
    Showers of blessing . . .

148   They shall come from the east

Words: John Gowans
Music: John Larsson

Andante con espress. ♩ = 72

1 They shall come from the east, they shall come from the west, and sit
2 They shall come from the east, they shall come from the west, and sit
3 They shall come from the east, they shall come from the west, and sit

down in the king - dom of God.   Both the rich and the poor, the des-
down in the king - dom of God,   to be met by their Fa - ther and
down in the king - dom of God.   Out of great tri - bu - la - tion to

- pised, the dis-tressed, they'll sit down in the king - dom of
wel - comed and blessed, and sit down in the king - dom of
tri - umph and rest, they'll sit down in the king - dom of

149 This is the mystery
(Let the bride say, 'Come!')

Words and music: Phil Lawson Johnston
and Chris Bowater

With strength

1 This is the mys - te - ry, that Christ has cho - sen you and me __ to
2 She's crowned in splen - dour and a roy - al di - a - dem; the
3 Now hear the Bride-groom call, 'Be - lov - ed, come a - side; the

be the re - ve - la - tion of His glo - ry;
King is __ en - thralled by her beau - ty.
time of __ be - troth - al is at hand. __

a cho - sen, roy - al, ho - ly peo - ple, set a - part and loved, a
A - dorned in right - eous - ness, ar - rayed __ in glo - rious light, the bride in
Lift up your eyes and see the dawn - ing of the day when as

150 Through the night of doubt and sorrow

ALL FOR JESUS   87 87

Words: Bernhardt S Ingemann (1789–1862)
tr. S Baring-Gould (1834–1924)
Music: John Stainer (1840–1901)
arranged Roger Mayor

1 Through the night of doubt and sor-row
2 Clear be-fore us through the dark-ness
3 One the light of God's own pres-ence
4 One the ob-ject of our jour-ney,

on - ward goes the pil-grim band,
gleams and burns the guid-ing light;
o'er His ran-somed peo-ple shed,
one the faith which ne - ver tires,

sing - ing songs of ex - pec - ta - tion,
bro - ther clasps the hand of bro-ther,
chas - ing far the gloom and ter - ror,
one the earn - est look-ing for-ward,

march - ing to the prom - ised land.
step - ping fear-less through the night.
bright-ening all the path we tread.
one the hope our   God in-spires.

This hymn may also be sung to ST OSWALD, *Combined Mission Praise* 338.

Music arrangement: © Roger Mayor / Jubilate Hymns

1 Through the night of doubt and sorrow
   onward goes the pilgrim band,
   singing songs of expectation,
   marching to the promised land.

2 Clear before us through the darkness
   gleams and burns the guiding light;
   brother clasps the hand of brother,
   stepping fearless through the night.

3 One the light of God's own presence
   o'er His ransomed people shed,
   chasing far the gloom and terror,
   brightening all the path we tread.

4 One the object of our journey,
   one the faith which never tires,
   one the earnest looking forward,
   one the hope our God inspires.

5 One the strain that lips of thousands
   lift as from the heart of one:
   one the conflict, one the peril,
   one the march in God begun.

6 One the gladness of rejoicing
   on the far eternal shore,
   where the one almighty Father
   reigns in love for evermore.

7 Onward, therefore, pilgrim brothers,
   onward with the cross our aid;
   bear its shame, and fight its battles,
   'til we rest beneath its shade.

8 Soon shall come the great awaking,
   soon the rending of the tomb;
   then the scattering of the shadows,
   and the end of toil and gloom.

151   Thy kingdom come, O God!

ST CECILIA   66 66

Words: L Hensley (1824–1905)
Music: L G Hayne (1836–83)

1 Thy king - dom come, O God, Thy
2 Where is Thy reign of peace and
3 When comes the pro - mised time that

rule, O Christ, be - gin; break with Thine i - ron
pu - ri - ty and love? When shall all hat - red
war shall be no more, and lust, op - pres - sion,

rod the ty - ran - nies of sin.
cease, as in the realms a - bove?
crime shall flee Thy face be - fore?

4 We pray Thee, Lord, arise,
    and come in Thy great might;
    revive our longing eyes,
    which languish for Thy sight.

5 Men scorn Thy sacred name,
    and wolves devour Thy fold;
    by many deeds of shame
    we learn that love grows cold.

6 O'er heathen lands afar
    thick darkness broodeth yet:
    arise, O Morning Star.
    Arise and never set.

152 Thy way, not mine, O Lord

IBSTONE 66 66

Words: H Bonar (1808–89)
Music: M Tiddeman (1837–1915)

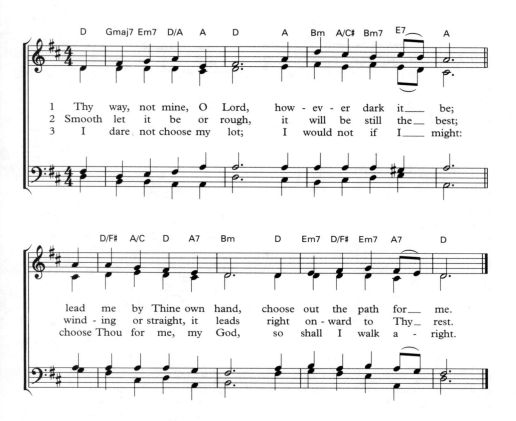

1 Thy way, not mine, O Lord, how-ev-er dark it__ be;
2 Smooth let it be or rough, it will be still the__ best;
3 I dare not choose my lot; I would not if I__ might:

lead me by Thine own hand, choose out the path for__ me.
wind-ing or straight, it leads right on-ward to Thy__ rest.
choose Thou for me, my God, so shall I walk a-right.

4 The kingdom that I seek
   is Thine; so let the way
   that leads to it be Thine,
   else I must surely stray.

5 Take Thou my cup, and it
   with joy or sorrow fill,
   as best to Thee may seem;
   choose Thou my good and ill.

6 Choose Thou for me my friends,
   my sickness or my health;
   choose Thou my cares for me,
   my poverty or wealth.

7 Not mine, not mine, the choice
   in things or great or small;
   be Thou my guide, my strength,
   my wisdom, and my all.

153

To be in Your presence
(My desire)

Words and music: Noel Richards
Music arranged David Peacock
and Geoff Twigg

Sensitively

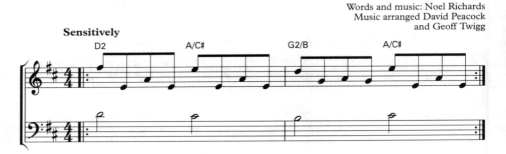

1 To be in Your pres - ence,
2 To rest in Your pres - ence,

to sit at Your feet,_____
not rush - ing a - way,_____

where Your love sur - rounds me,
to cher - ish each mo - ment —

and makes me＿ com - plete:＿＿＿＿＿   this is my de -
here I＿ would stay:＿＿＿＿＿

- sire,   O＿ Lord,   this is my de - sire.

This is my de - sire,   O＿ Lord,   this is my de -

- sire.

154   Touch my life

Words and music: Derek Bond
arranged L Hills

1 Touch my life, O___ Lord___ my God; ho-ly fire,___ come.
2 Touch my heart, O___ Lord___ my God, cleanse me with Your blood.

— Touch my lips___ that___ I___ might speak of the won-
— Fill me with___ Your___ Spi - rit, Lord, flow through___

1.
- ders of___ Your Son.___
_ me like___ a flood.

2.
— Your Spi-rit's a - noint - ing I___ des - ire:

the pow-er of God. — To de-mon-strate jus - tice, Lord, I need

the pow-er of God. — To tell of Your heal - ing and — re - lease,

the pow-er of God. —

1 Touch my life, O Lord my God;
  holy fire, come.
  Touch my lips that I might speak
  of the wonders of Your Son.

2 Touch my heart, O Lord my God,
  cleanse me with Your blood.
  Fill me with Your Spirit, Lord,
  flow through me like a flood.
    Your Spirit's anointing I desire:
    the power of God.
    To demonstrate justice, Lord, I need
    the power of God.
    To tell of Your healing and release,
    the power of God.

155 To Your majesty

Words and music: Sue Rinaldi
and Steve Bassett

To Your maj-es-ty___ and Your beau-ty I___ sur-ren - der,___
to Your ho-li-ness and Your love I sur-ren - der,___
for You are_ an awe-some God who is migh - ty, You de-
- serve_____ my deep-est praise: with all of my heart, with
all of my life,___ I sur-ren - der.___

156

We are marching
(Siyahamba)

Words: African origin, collected and edited by Anders Nyberg
English verses 2 and 3: Andrew Maries
Music: African melody scored by Notman KB,
Ljungsbro and Lars Parkman

2 We are living in the love of God . . .

3 We are moving in the power of God . . .

157 We are His children

Words and music: Graham Kendrick

With life

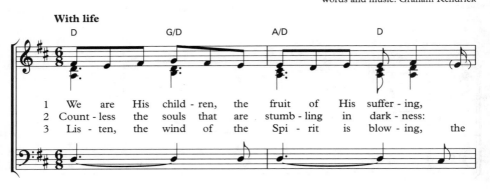

1 We are His child - ren, the fruit of His suffer - ing,
2 Count - less the souls that are stumb - ling in dark - ness:
3 Lis - ten, the wind of the Spi - rit is blow - ing, the

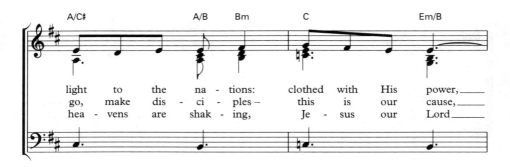

saved and re-deemed by His blood; called to be ho - ly, a
why do we sleep in the light? Je - sus com-mands us to
end of the age is so near; powers in the earth and the

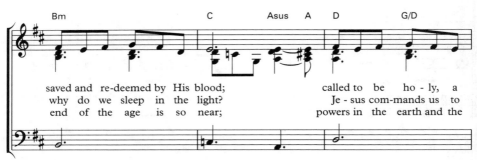

light to the na - tions: clothed with His power,____
go, make dis - ci - ples – this is our cause,____
hea - vens are shak - ing, Je - sus our Lord____

____ filled with His love.____
____ this is our fight.____
____ soon shall ap - pear!____

Go forth in His name, pro - claim - ing

'Je - sus reigns!' Now is the time_ for the Church to a - rise and pro -

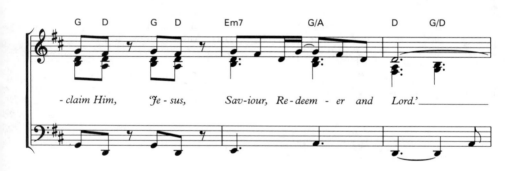

- claim Him, 'Je - sus, Sav - iour, Re - deem - er and Lord.'_

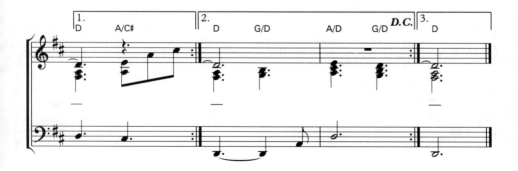

158 We turn to Christ alone

DINBYCH   DSM

Words: Timothy Dudley-Smith
Music: J Parry (1841–1903)

1 We turn to Christ alone, the
2 We turn from self and sin in
3 We turn from ev - ery wrong, from
4 We turn to Christ as Lord who

Son of God di - vine, to bow the knee be -
pe - ni - tence and shame; we trust, to make us
ev - ery e - vil way, who in the Spi - rit's
died and rose a - gain, as those whose hearts re -

- fore His throne, to bear His name and
clean with - in, the power of Je - sus'
strength are strong, as child - ren of the
- ceive His word, as sub - jects of His

159 We want to see Jesus lifted high

Words and music: Doug Horley

Lively ♩ = 160

We want to see Je - sus lift - ed high,__ a ban-ner that flies

__ a - cross this land,__ that all men might see__ the truth and know

__ He is the way__ to Hea - ven.

We want to see,
We're gon-na see,

we want to see,
we're gon-na see,

we want to see Je - sus lift - ed high,
we're gon-na see Je - sus lift - ed high,

we want to see, we want to see, we want to see Je -
we're gon-na see, we're gon-na see we're gon-na see Je -

- sus lift - ed high.__ Step by step we're mov-ing for - ward, lit-tle by

lit-tle tak - ing ground, ev - ery prayer a pow-er-ful wea - pon, strong-holds

come tum-bl - ing down__ and down and down__ and down.

160 Welcome, King of kings

Words and music: Noel Richards

Brightly, with strength

Wel - come,_ King of kings! How great_ is Your name! You come_ in maj - es - ty_ for ev - er_ to reign.

1 You rule the
2 Let all cre -

na - tions, they shake at the sound of_ Your
-a - tion_ bow down at the sound of_ Your

name – to You is giv - en___ all power,
name. Let ev - ery tongue now___ con - fess

and You shall reign.
the Lord God reigns.

D.C.

Welcome, King of kings!
How great is Your name!
You come in majesty
for ever to reign.

1 You rule the nations,
   they shake at the sound of Your name–
   to You is given all power,
   and You shall reign.
      Welcome, King of kings . . .

2 Let all creation bow down
   at the sound of Your name.
   Let every tongue now confess
   the Lord God reigns.
      Welcome, King of kings . . .

161

What kind of greatness

Words and music: Graham Kendrick

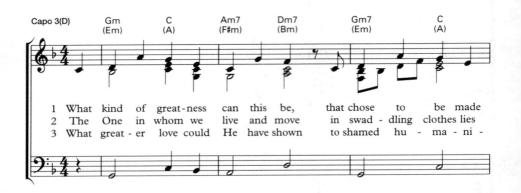

1 What kind of great-ness can this be, that chose to be made small,
2 The One in whom we live and move in swad - dling clothes lies bound.
3 What great - er love could He have shown to shamed hu - ma - ni - ty?

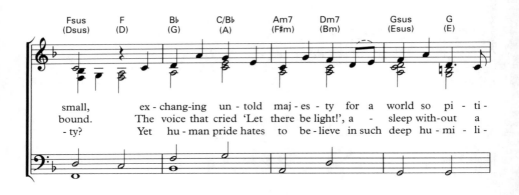

small, ex - chang-ing un - told maj - es - ty for a world so pi - ti -
bound. The voice that cried 'Let there be light!', a - sleep with-out a
- ty? Yet hu - man pride hates to be - lieve in such deep hu - mi - li -

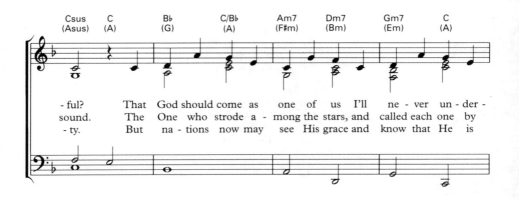

- ful? That God should come as one of us I'll ne - ver un - der -
sound. The One who strode a - mong the stars, and called each one by
- ty. But na - tions now may see His grace and know that He is

162 Whatever is true

Words and music: Brian Doerksen
and Craig Musseau

Steadily ♩ = 70

What-ev-er is true, what-ev-er is right, what-ev-er is

pure, what-ev-er is love - ly, we __ will

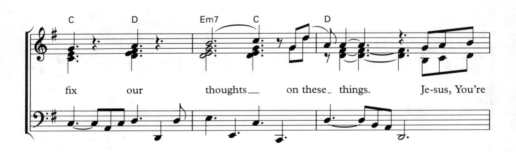

fix our thoughts __ on these _ things. Je-sus, You're

true, Je-sus, You're right, Je-sus, You're

like_ You?_

like_ You?_

What-ev-er is

last time

who is like You, who is like You?_

like_ You,___

who is like You?_

Whatever is true, whatever is right,
whatever is pure, whatever is lovely,
we will fix our thoughts on these things.
Jesus, You're true, Jesus, You're right,
Jesus, You're pure, You are lovely.
We will fix our thoughts on You.

MEN	Jesus,
WOMEN	Jesus,
MEN	who is like You,
WOMEN	who is like You?
MEN	Jesus,
WOMEN	Jesus,
MEN	who is like You,
WOMEN	who is like You?
MEN	Jesus . . .
ALL	who is like You?

163   When I lift up my voice

Words: from Psalm 142
Michael Perry
Music: Chris Rolinson

Lightly Latin feel

1 When I lift up my voice, and I cry to the Lord,
2 Then He'll come to my side and He'll ans-wer my prayers,

— and I pour out my trou - bles be -
— and He'll set my soul free from its

- fore Him; when I see no - one cares,
pri - son; then the right-eous will see

— and I walk all a - lone,
— and they'll ga - ther a - round

and my spi-rit grows wea - ry___ with-in___ me,___ then I sing:
all be-cause of His good - ness___ to-wards me.___ Then they'll sing:

'You are my re - fuge,___ I will praise Your
'You are our re - fuge,___ we will praise Your

name; You are so good to me,___ O
name; You are so good to us,___ O

Lord!'_____ Then I sing: 'You are my re -
Lord!'_____ Then they'll sing: 'You are our re -

- fuge, — 　　　　I 　will praise 　Your 　name;
- fuge, — 　　　　we 　will praise 　Your 　name;

You 　are 　so 　good 　to 　me, _____ You 　are 　so
You 　are 　so 　good 　to 　us, _____ You 　are 　so

good 　to 　me, _____ You 　are 　so 　good 　to 　me, — O ___
good 　to 　us, _____ You 　are 　so 　good 　to 　us, — O ___

Lord!' _____ —

When my sorrows cover me

Words: from Psalm 69
Michael Perry
Music: Chris Rolinson

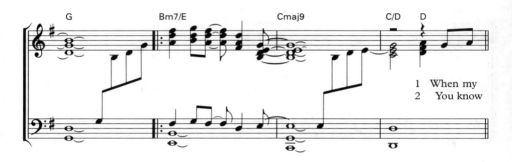

1 When my
2 You know

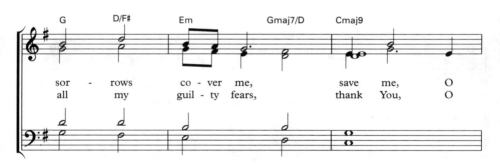

sor - rows co - ver me, save me, O
all my guil - ty fears, thank You, O

God; when my friends a - ban-don me, when I seek what
God. You have heard with o - pen ears, You have seen my

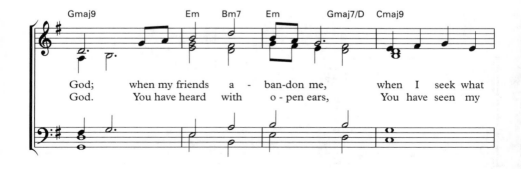

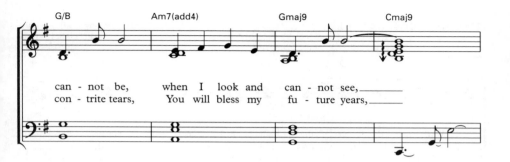

can - not be,   when I look and   can - not see,_____
con - trite tears,   You will bless my   fu - ture years,_____

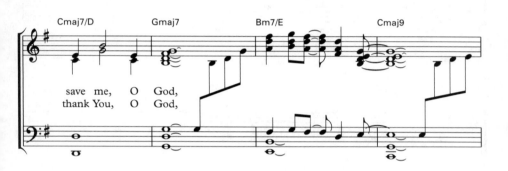

save me,   O God,
thank You,   O God,

save me,   O   God.
thank You,   O   God,

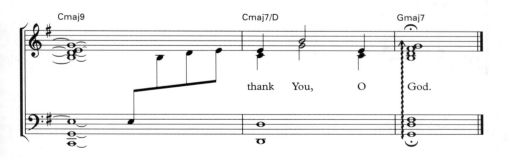

thank   You,   O   God.

165 With undivided heart

HILLCREST   10 4 10 4 66 64

Words: Timothy Dudley-Smith
Music: Greg Leavers

1 With un - di - vi - ded heart and cease - less songs give___ thanks to God.___ To Him all maj - es - ty and praise be - longs: give_ thanks to God. His love and truth pro -
2 Ex - alt His name and His e - ter - nal word, He___ is our God.___ Be - fore His throne our ev - ery prayer is heard, He_ is our God. Let kings de - clare His
3 He reigns in glo - ry from His throne a - bove, He___ is the Lord,___ and in our weak - ness meets us with His love: He_ is the Lord. His pur - pose can - not

1 With undivided heart and ceaseless songs
   give thanks to God.
   To Him all majesty and praise belongs:
   give thanks to God.
   His love and truth proclaim,
   His mercy still the same;
   and for His holy name
   give thanks to God.

2 Exalt His name and His eternal word,
   He is our God.
   Before His throne our every prayer is heard,
   He is our God.
   Let kings declare His praise,
   sing of His words and ways,
   for through eternal days
   He is our God.

3 He reigns in glory from His throne above,
   He is the Lord,
   and in our weakness meets us with His love:
   He is the Lord.
   His purpose cannot fail;
   though fears and foes assail,
   His love shall still prevail,
   He is the Lord.

166

With all my heart

Words and music: Roger Mayor

With all my heart I'll sing prai - ses to You my King,

with all my be - ing, ex - alt Your name!

Words ne - ver can ex-press my heart-felt thank-ful-ness,

but this I now con-fess, 'I love You,____ Lord.'
'I'll serve You,____ Lord.'

167 Wonderful counsellor

Words and music: Chick Yuill

Moderato ♩ = 108

1 Won - der - ful coun - sel - lor, migh - ty God a - mong us,
2 Son of God, Son of Man, Word of God in - car - nate,
3 King of kings, Lord of lords, Son of God ex - alt - ed;

ev - er - last - ing Fa - ther, Prince who rules in peace. To_
suf - fering Sav - iour, glo - ri - ous ris - en_ Lord. For_
name a - bove_ ev - ery name, Lamb up - on the throne. This

us a child is born, to us a son is given, to
God so loved the world He gave His on - ly son; no
king will come a - gain, the Fa - ther's on - ly son; no

those who walked in dark-ness the light has come.
more we walk in dark-ness, the light has come.
more a world in dark-ness, the light will come.

168 Wonderful grace

Words and music: John Pantry
Music arranged Christopher Norton

1 Won-der-ful grace that gives what I don't de-serve, pays me what Christ has earned, then lets me go___ free. Won-der-ful grace that gives me the time to change, wash-es a-

2 Won-der-ful love that held in the face of death, breathed in its la-test breath for-give-ness for___ me. Won-der-ful love, whose power can break ev-ery chain, giv-ing us

1 Wonderful grace
   that gives what I don't deserve,
   pays me what Christ has earned,
   then lets me go free.
   Wonderful grace
   that gives me the time to change,
   washes away the stains
   that once covered me.
     And all that I have
     I lay at the feet
     of the wonderful Saviour
     who loves me.

2 Wonderful love
   that held in the face of death,
   breathed in its latest breath
   forgiveness for me.
   Wonderful love,
   whose power can break every chain,
   giving us life again
   and setting us free.
     And all that I have . . .

169   Years I spent in vanity and pride
(At Calvary)

Words: W R Newell (1868–1956)
Music: D B Towner (1850–1919)

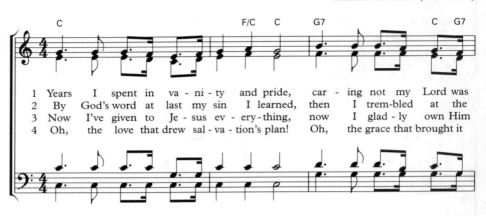

1 Years   I   spent in   va - ni - ty   and pride,   car - ing not my   Lord was
2 By   God's word at   last my sin   I learned,   then   I   trem-bled   at   the
3 Now   I've given to   Je - sus ev - ery-thing,   now   I   glad - ly   own Him
4 Oh,   the   love that drew sal - va - tion's plan!   Oh,   the grace that brought it

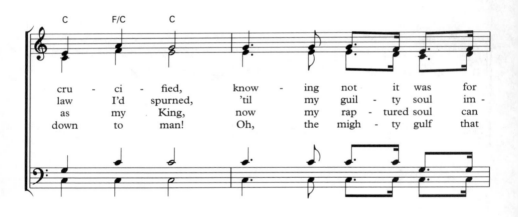

cru - ci - fied,   know - ing   not   it   was   for
law   I'd   spurned,   'til   my   guil - ty   soul   im -
as   my   King,   now   my   rap - tured soul   can
down   to   man!   Oh,   the   migh - ty   gulf   that

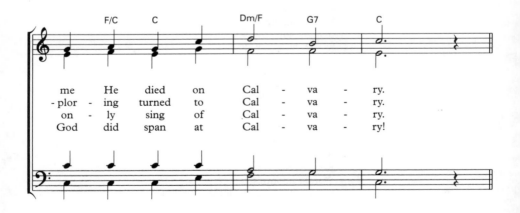

me   He   died   on   Cal - va - ry.
- plor - ing   turned   to   Cal - va - ry.
on - ly   sing   of   Cal - va - ry.
God   did   span   at   Cal - va - ry!

Mer - cy there was great and grace was free, par - don there was mul - ti - plied to me,

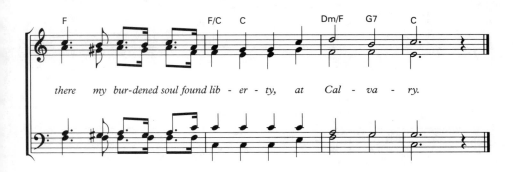

there my bur-dened soul found lib - er - ty, at Cal - va - ry.

1 Years I spent in vanity and pride,
   caring not my Lord was crucified,
   knowing not it was for me He died on Calvary.
   Mercy there was great and grace was free,
   pardon there was multiplied to me,
   there my burdened soul found liberty,
   at Calvary.

2 By God's word at last my sin I learned,
   then I trembled at the law I'd spurned,
   'til my guilty soul imploring turned to Calvary.
   Mercy there was great . . .

3 Now I've given to Jesus everything,
   now I gladly own Him as my King,
   now my raptured soul can only sing of Calvary.
   Mercy there was great . . .

4 Oh, the love that drew salvation's plan!
   Oh, the grace that brought it down to man!
   Oh, the mighty gulf that God did span at Calvary!
   Mercy there was great . . .

170

You are the rock
(Triumph of Your grace)

Words and music: Steve Chua
Music arranged Daniel Chua

1 You are the rock on which we stand,
2 Se - cure and stead - fast in Your love,
(3) fash-ioned by the pat - tern of this world, we

we place our lives in - to Your hands, at the
we stand in the pow - er of Your blood, with Your
take our cross and Je - sus we will serve, as we

foot of the cross we ac - know-ledge You as Lord,
Spi - rit of truth a - noint-ing our des - ire to
of - fer our lives as a ho - ly sac - ri - fice, re -

171 You did not wait for me
(I'm for ever grateful)

Words and music: Mark Altrogge

You did not wait for me to draw near to You,
but You clothed Yourself in frail humanity.
You did not wait for me to cry out to You,
but You let me hear Your voice calling me,
and I'm for ever grateful to You,
I'm for ever grateful for the cross,
I'm for ever grateful to You,
that You came to seek and save the lost.

172   You make my heart feel glad

Words and music: Patricia Morgan
and Sue Rinaldi

With a steady rock rhythm ♩ = 160

You make my heart feel___ glad,___

You make my heart feel___ glad,___

Je - sus, You bring me___ joy,___

You make my heart feel___ glad.___

173 You have been given

Words and music: Bob Kauflin

1 You have been giv-en__ the name a-bove all names, and we wor - ship
2 We are Your peo-ple,__ made for Your glo-ry, and we wor - ship
3 You have re-deemed us__ from ev-ery na-tion and we wor - ship

You, yes, we wor - ship You. You have been giv-en__ the
You, yes, we wor - ship You. We are Your peo-ple,__
You, yes, we wor - ship You. You have re-deemed us__

name a-bove all names, and we wor - ship You,
made for Your glo-ry, and we wor - ship You,
from ev-ery na-tion and we wor - ship You,

yes, we wor - ship You.

last time

174   Yours for ever! God of love

NEWINGTON   77 77

Words: M F Maude (1819–1913)
Music: W D Maclagan (1826–1910)

1 Yours for ev - er! God of love, hear us from Your throne a - bove;
2 Yours for ev - er! Lord of life, shield us through our earth - ly strife;
3 Yours for ev - er! O how blessed they who find in You their rest!

Yours for ev - er may we be, ___ here and in e - ter - ni - ty.
You the life, the truth, the way, ___ guide us to the realms of day.
Sav - iour, guard-ian, heaven-ly friend, O de-fend us to the end.

1 Yours for ever! God of love,
  hear us from Your throne above;
  Yours for ever may we be,
  here and in eternity.

2 Yours for ever! Lord of life,
  shield us through our earthly strife;
  You the life, the truth, the way,
  guide us to the realms of day.

3 Yours for ever! O how blessed
  they who find in You their rest!
  Saviour, guardian, heavenly friend,
  O defend us to the end.

4 Yours for ever! Shepherd, keep
  us Your frail and trembling sheep;
  safe alone beneath Your care,
  let us all Your goodness share.

5 Yours for ever! You our guide,
  all our wants by You supplied,
  all our sins by You forgiven,
  lead us, Lord, from earth to Heaven.

Copyright Addresses

Ateliers et Presses de Taizé, Taizé Community, F 71250, France

Bridge, Basil E, 124 Linacre Avenue, Sprowston, Norwich, Norfolk NR7 8JS

CopyCare Ltd, PO Box 77, Hailsham, East Sussex BN27 3EF

Daybreak Music Ltd, Silverdale Road, Eastbourne, East Sussex BN20 7AB

Dudley-Smith, Timothy, 9 Ashlands, Ford, Salisbury, Wiltshire SP4 6DY

Ellel Ministries Ltd, Ellel Grange, Ellel, Lancaster LA2 OHN

Evans, Dilys, Tan-y-Coed, Uxbridge Square, Caernarfon, Gwynedd LL55 2RE

Haynes, Stuart, 4 Magdalen Way, Worle, Weston-super-Mare BS22 OPG

Hope Publishing Company, 380 South Main Place, Carol Stream, IL 60188, USA

Iona Community, Pearce Institute, 840 Govan Road, Glasgow G51 3UU

John Ireland Trust, 35 St Mary's Mansions, St Mary's Terrace, London W2 1SQ

Jubilate Hymns, c/o Mrs Bunty Grundy, 61 Chessel Avenue, Southampton SO19 4DY

Kingsway's Thankyou Music, PO Box 75, Eastbourne, East Sussex BN23 6NW

Leavers, Greg, 1 Haws Hill, Carnforth, Lancashire LA5 9DD

Make Way Music, PO Box 263, Croydon, Surrey CR9 5AP

OCP Publications, 5536 NE Hassolo, Portland, OR 97213, USA

Oxford University Press (Hymn Copyright Department), 3 Park Road, London NW1 6XN

PolyGram International Music Publishing Ltd, Bond House, 347–353 Chiswick High Road, Chiswick, London W4 4HS

Public Trust Office, Stewart House, 24 Kingsway, London WC2B 6JX

Salvationist Publishing and Supplies, 117-121 Judd Street, King's Cross, London WC1H 9NN

Serious Music UK, 11 Junction Road, Oldfield Park, Bath, Avon BA2 3NQ

Sound Impression, 44 Adelaide Road, Chichester, West Sussex PO19 4NF

Sovereign Lifestyle Music, PO Box 356, Leighton Buzzard, Beds LU7 8WP

Sovereign Music UK, PO Box 356, Leighton Buzzard, Beds LU7 8WP

Spiller, Lawson, Ivy Cottage, 36 High Street, Claverham, Avon BS19 4NE

Stainer & Bell Ltd, PO Box 110, Victoria House, 23 Gruneisen Road, Finchley, London N3 1DZ

Tehillah Trust, 49 St Mary's Park, Nailsea, Bristol BS19 2RP

Windswept Pacific Music, 27 Queensdale Place, London W11 4SQ

Using *New Mission Praise*

New Mission Praise contains a range of hymns and songs suitable for both choirs and music groups. SATB arrangements are listed in the SATB index below, and modern arrangements of traditional hymn tunes are cross-referenced to the SATB versions available in **Mission Praise Combined**. Some of the items may prove more suitable as performance items than for congregational singing, depending on the size and musical strength of the local church.

Every item includes guitar/keyboard chords above the stave. It should be noted that many of the keyboard arrangements are intended as outline accompaniments only, and more enterprising players should feel free to elaborate on these or to adapt them in a style appropriate to their local situation.

A guitar chord chart appears overleaf, listing over 150 of the most commonly used chords in the book. In many items capo markings have been provided to simplify the arrangements. Capo 3(D), for example, means that the capo should be placed at the third fret, and the chords in brackets should then be played.

Other points to note:

- Chords marked 'sus' are 'sus4' chords.

- Chords may be simplified by omitting 7ths, 9ths and so on, e.g. for Cm7, play Cm, for C2, play C, for Csus, play C, for C9, play C, or by omitting the suggested bass note, e.g. for D/A play D.

- The more traditional hymn tunes contain rapid chord changes and may be more suited to keyboard-only accompaniment. If a keyboard is not available, guitarists may wish to experiment with omitting some of the chords.

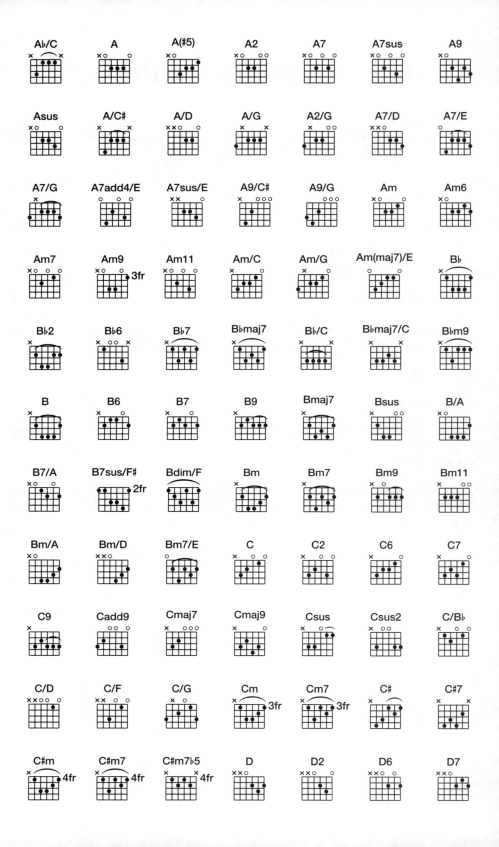

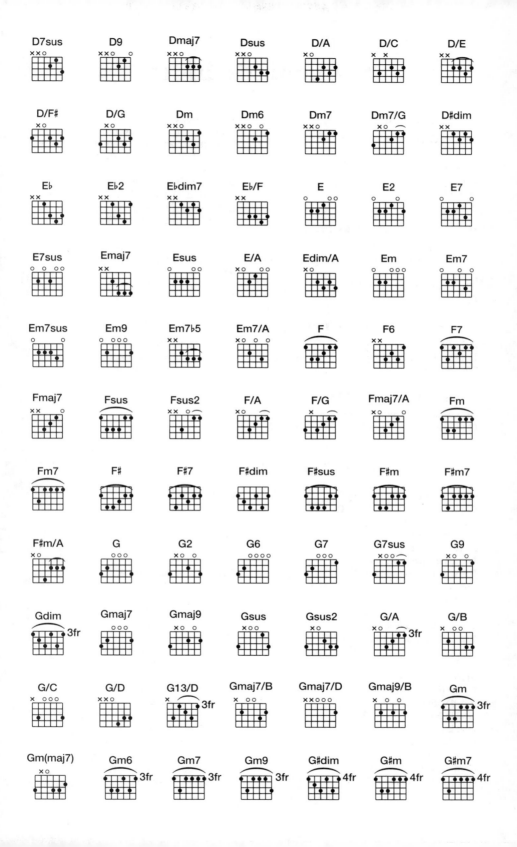

Thematic Index

A. The Godhead

God in Glory and Majesty
God the Creator
God the Father
Jesus - God the Son
The Holy Spirit
The Trinity

B. The Church of Jesus Christ

Unity of the Church
Outreach of the Church - Evangelism and
 Mission
The Scriptures
Communion

C. Seasons of the Church Year

Advent and Christmas
Easter and Holy Week
The Return of Christ

D. Living the Christian Life

Praise and Thanksgiving
Celebration

Proclamation
Worship and Adoration
Confession and Repentance
Commitment and Dedication to Service
Prayer
Revival and Personal Renewal
Faith and Trust in God
Salvation and the Cross
Devotion and Love for God
Guidance
Comfort, Strength and Security
Health, Healing and Deliverance
Trials and Temptations
Spiritual Warfare
Heaven and Victory over Death

E. Other Subjects

Morning and Evening
Blessings and Doxologies
Songs Suitable for Children

Section A: The Godhead

God in Glory and Majesty
Come, let us worship Jesus - 18
God is great - 38
He is the Lord - 45
Holy and majestic - 47
Jesus is the name we honour - 72
Jesus, restore to us again - 75
Lord God almighty - 80
Lord of lords - 85
Mighty God - 92
With undivided heart - 165
You make my heart feel glad - 172

God the Creator
Eternal God - 24
Father of creation - 28
Filled with compassion - 30
God in His love for us - 34
God is great - 38
He is the Lord - 45
I, the Lord of sea and sky - 59
Lord God almighty - 80
O Lord, the refuge - 111

Oh, I was made for this - 114
Out of a heart of love - 118
Praise the Lord, you heavens - 122
Teach me to dance - 138

God the Father
Beauty for brokenness - 8
Faithful God - 26
Faithful One - 27
Father of heaven - 29
God has spoken - 33
Holy and majestic - 47
I should be getting to know You - 56
No-one but You, Lord - 101
O Father of the fatherless - 108
O God of Bethel - 109
O Lord, the refuge - 111

Jesus - God the Son
All I once held dear - 1
And He shall reign - 4
At the foot of the cross - 7
Beauty for brokenness - 8

The Holy Spirit

The Trinity

Section B: The Church of Jesus Christ

Unity of the Church

Outreach of the Church - Evangelism and Mission

We want to see Jesus lifted high - 159
What kind of greatness - 161

The Scriptures
God has spoken - 33
Jesus, Jesus, holy and anointed One - 74
Jesus, restore to us again - 75
More about Jesus - 91

Now in reverence and awe - 104
Open our eyes, Lord - 117

Communion
Here is bread, here is wine - 44
In the streets of every city - 68
Sweet feast of love divine - 136
The love of God comes close - 142

Section C: Seasons of the Church Year

Advent and Christmas
Rumours of angels - 124
Since the day the angel came - 130
So many centuries - 133
What kind of greatness - 161
Wonderful counsellor - 167

Easter and Holy Week
At the foot of the cross - 7
Christ is risen - 14
He has risen - 41
Heaven's throne ascending - 42
I know a place - 53

Now is Christ risen from the dead - 103
O Christ, the King of glory - 107
Thank You for saving me - 139

The Return of Christ
And He shall reign - 4
Beauty for brokenness - 8
Father of creation - 28
Great is the darkness - 37
I want to serve the purpose of God - 61
Sing a song of celebration - 132
Thy kingdom come, O God - 151
We are His children - 157

Section D: Living the Christian Life

Praise and Thanksgiving
As water to the thirsty - 5
At the foot of the cross - 7
Beauty for brokenness - 8
Blessèd be the name of the Lord - 10
Blessèd be the name of the Lord - 22
Great is God - 36
God is great - 38
I love to hear the story - 55
In the Lord I'll be ever thankful - 67
Jesus is the name we honour - 72
Let the song go round the earth - 78
Lord God almighty - 80
Lord, I lift Your name on high - 83
Lord of lords - 85
My heart is full of admiration - 95
My life is in You, Lord - 97
My lips shall praise You - 98
No other name - 100
Nothing shall separate us - 102
O Lord, I want to sing Your praises - 106
O Lord, the refuge - 111
O Lord, whose saving name - 112
O spread the tidings - 113
Praise the Lord, you heavens - 122
See His glory - 127
Shout for joy and sing - 129
Sing to the Lord a joyful song - 131

Standing on the promises - 134
Teach me to dance - 138
Welcome, King of kings - 160
When I lift up my voice - 163
When my sorrows cover me - 164
With undivided heart - 165
With all my heart - 166
You are the rock - 170
You make my heart feel glad - 172

Celebration
Down the mountain - 23
He has risen - 41
How wonderful - 51
Jesus Christ is the Lord of all - 73
O Lord, I want to sing Your praises - 106
O Lord, whose saving name - 112
Sing a song of celebration - 132

Proclamation
Called to a battle - 13
Christ is risen - 14
Father of creation - 28
Filled with compassion - 30
God has chosen me - 32
How do we start - 49
How wonderful - 51
I am persuaded - 52

Section E: Other Subjects

Bible Index

Malachi

3:2	123
4:2	113

Matthew

1:23	93
2:11	130
5:6	121
6:9-13	119
6:10	28, 108, 139, 151
6:11	109
6:25	109
6:31	109
6:33	152
7:13-14	88, 152
7:15	151
8:3	145
8:11	148
8:24	88
9:36	30
11:5	15
13:35	28
14:14	8
14:41	121
15:31	68
16:24	170
17:3	75
18:3	138
18:12	108
19:14	112
20:28	29
22:37	166
24:35	4
25:34	28
25:38	142
26:26	44, 136
26:42	108
26:64	4
27:29	7
27:33	7
27:51	121
28:6	14, 15, 41, 103
28:7	103
28:19	13, 37, 87, 157

Mark

1:15	61
4:37	88
6:34	30
8:34	137, 170
10:28	29
10:45	143
11:28	153
12:30	166
13:26	4
14:3	21
14:20	44
14:22	136
14:25	44
14:62	4
15:7	7
15:23	130
15:24	7
15:38	121
16:6	14, 15, 41, 103

Luke

1:26	130
1:33	4
1:35	20
1:75	46
1:78	21
2:4-7	130
2:7	161
2:9-14	55
2:12	161
2:13-14	130
2:14	85
2:19	130
2:32	21
2:51	130
3:16	20
4	32
6:20	8
7:22	15
7:37	21
8:1	61
8:5	117
8:23	88
9:2	61
9:23	137, 170
9:27	61
9:30	75
9:60	157
10:9	61
10:18	14
10:30	7
11:1	86
11:2	28, 139
11:2-4	119
11:3	109
11:5	151
12:22	109
12:31	152
13:18	61
13:24	88
13:29	148
14:15	61
14:28	141
15:4	108
15:20	114
18:7	62
18:17	61
19:10	15, 30, 42, 171
22:18	44
22:19	136
22:42	108
23:33	7, 169
23:34	130
23:42	12
23:43	130
23:45	121
24:6	14, 15, 41, 103
24:30	44
24:32	140

John

1:1	33
1:14	29, 75, 127, 167
3:3	65
3:7	65
3:8	157
3:16	167
3:19	167
3:29	132
4:42	139
5:21	108
6:31	59
6:33	108
6:41	59
6:50	59
6:58	59
6:63	108
7:37	69
8:28	159
8:32	139
10:11-14	57, 130
10:11-18	90
10:27	174
10:28	108
10:38	136
12:3	21
12:15	141
12:32	159, 170
13:1	57
14:2	96, 109
14:6	112, 117, 159, 174
14:7	136
14:9	136
14:16	113
14:16-17	170
14:17	75
14:24	75
14:26	113
14:27	99
15:16	64
15:26	75
16:13	75
17:2	108
19:5	7
19:18	7
19:25	7
19:39	130

Metrical Index

Index to Tunes

Index of items suitable for SATB

SATB arrangement available in Combined Mission Praise

Main Index

Titles which differ from first lines are shown in italics.

Other *Mission Praise* titles available from HarperCollins:

Mission Praise
0 551 01091 6	Words only A5 single copy (paperback)
0 551 01087 8	Words only A5 50 copy pack
0 551 01281 1	Words only Large Print (paperback)
0 551 01413 X	Music (hardback)

Mission Praise 2
0 551 01590 X	Words only A5 single copy (paperback)
0 551 01417 2	Words only A5 50 copy pack
0 551 01416 4	Music (hardback)

Mission Praise Combined
0 551 01979 4	Words only (hardback)
0 551 01977 8	Words only 25 copy pack
0 551 02627 8	Words only Easy-to-read (hardback)
0 551 01978 6	Words only Large Print (paperback)
0 551 01986 7	Music (hardback)

Related titles:

Sing Mission Praise (vocal arrangements)
0 551 04010 6	Music (paperback)

Play Mission Praise (instrumental arrangements)
0 551 02954 4	Book 1 (paperback)
0 551 02955 3	Book 2 (paperback)

For further details please contact your local HarperCollins office.